SHELTON STATE
COLLEGE
JUNIOR COLLEGE
LIBRARY

THOMAS HARDY AND HISTORY

By the same author

THE POLITICAL THOUGHT OF S. T. COLERIDGE
POLITICAL TRACTS OF WORDSWORTH, COLERIDGE AND SHELLEY
THE CONSERVATIVE TRADITION
FROM WATERLOO TO PETERLOO
CAMBRIDGE LIFE
LIFE IN REGENCY ENGLAND
EUROPE IN THE EIGHTEENTH CENTURY
DR. BENTLEY
THE AGE OF GEORGE THE THIRD
THE ANTI-PHILOSOPHERS

Novels

THE SMARTEST GRAVE
THE WOMEN OF PEASENHALL
A SECOND-HAND TOMB

Thomas Hardy
and History

R. J. WHITE

We thank you, Sir, for all that you
have written . . . but most of all,
perhaps, for The Dynasts.

*An address to Thomas Hardy on his eighty-
first birthday from a hundred and six of the
younger writers of England (Life, p. 413)*

Discarded
SSCC

Macmillan

© Vera White 1974

All rights reserved. No part of this publication may be
reproduced or transmitted, in any form or by any means,
without permission.

First published 1974 by
THE MACMILLAN PRESS LTD
London and Basingstoke
Associated companies in New York
Dublin Melbourne Johannesburg and Madras

SBN 333 10288 6

Typeset by
COLD COMPOSITION LTD
Southborough, Tunbridge Wells
Printed in Great Britain by
LEWIS REPRINTS LTD.
Member of the Brown Knight & Truscott
(Holdings) Ltd. group of companies,
London and Tonbridge

Contents

Preface

R. J. White, the distinguished historian, writer and Fellow of Downing College, Cambridge, died in 1971. He had been a lifelong admirer of Hardy's work, and at the time of his death was writing a book which was to be the fruit of his deep interest in Hardy and in Hardy's use of history.

Sadly, he did not live to complete it, but enough had been written to make this present publication possible. My part in it has been to edit the material left to us in such a way that the perception, judgement and common sense which were so obviously present even in the unrevised and incomplete pages of the book could be presented in the most suitable form and thus give permanent expression to an outstanding historian's approach to literature.

In my work I have been greatly helped by R.J.'s widow, Mrs Vera White, to whom I express my sincere thanks.

JAMES GIBSON

1 Hardy and History

The climax of Hardy's lifelong fascination with history came with the publication of *The Dynasts* in the first decade of this century, but by that time he was in his sixties and already author of fourteen novels in which history had played its part. The scenes of these novels were spaced in time over most of the decades of the nineteenth century. The novelist had himself lived through most of them, and he had direct knowledge of the rest. Thus, he breaks into his description of Miller Loveday's 'little entertainment' in the fifth chapter of *The Trumpet-Major* with

> The present writer, to whom this party has been described times out of number by members of the Loveday family and other aged people now passed away, can never enter the old living-room of Overcombe Mill without beholding the genial scene through the mists of the seventy or eighty years that intervene between then and now.

He had not been present himself only because he had not yet been born. It was like his grandmother's recollections of the French Revolution. 'I remember', she said, and just as the small things recall the great, and *vice versa,* she remembered that she had been ironing her best muslin gown when the news came that the Queen of France had been beheaded. Nearly forty years after hearing these memories, which were to be enshrined in 1902 in his poem, 'One We Knew', Hardy made a note that Sir Frederick Pollock had mentioned that he had once danced in the same quadrille with a gentleman who had once danced with Marie Antoinette. One way or another Hardy never felt himself far removed from the Age of the Dynasts.

A great deal of what would now be accounted 'history' in the Wessex Novels was scarcely that to their author.

Characters, actions, ideas, often belonged to his own lifetime and could have formed part of his experience. Ethelberta Petherwin, Paula Power and Sue Bridehead all show what are, to the historian of nineteenth-century England, familiar features of the 'girl of the period' even the 'new woman'. The contrasts of *A Laodicean* — the medieval castle, the railway, the telephone — all belong considerably to the England of Lord Tennyson's 'Locksley Hall', 'Maud', and 'The Princess'. Hardy's picturing of these things should obviously go under the title 'How It Strikes a Contemporary'. Looking back from 1912 Hardy himself thought *The Hand of Ethelberta* (1876) had appeared thirty-five years too soon and that, by the time he wrote the Preface to the 1912 Wessex Edition, history had caught up with him. He was, indeed, more often ahead of than behind the times. He often gives the impression of writing his novels with the future historian in mind. He spaces them across the decades of the nineteenth century as carefully as Balzac located his novels among the various classes and professions of contemporary French society in his *Comédie Humaine.* They span the century decade by decade, from the time when preparations were made against the landing of the French in *The Trumpet-Major,* down to the death of Tess Durbeyfield in the late 1880s. Like the historically-minded man he was, Hardy never leaves us in any doubt where we are, or where his 'poor puppets' were, in terms of time, even if our attention is more generally focused on the easy and obvious question of their location in space.

The opening of *The Mayor of Casterbridge* is typical of his unequivocal procedures:

> One evening of late summer, before the present century had reached its thirtieth year, a young man and woman, the latter carrying a child, were approaching the large village of Weydon-Priors, in Upper Wessex, on foot.

Edmund Blunden has described this as no heaven-sent opening for a novel and referred to Hardy's 'dragging sentences' and 'stuffy wordings'[1] but this criticism is regardless of the fact that the passage has a purely informative purpose and is wonderfully appropriate to the weary walk of people nearing the end of a long day's trudge. When he supplied a Preface in 1895 Hardy begged the reader to bear in mind that his story relates to the days when the home corn trade was all-important and everyone was vitally concerned with the harvest weather. And with typical devotion to historic fact he vouches for there having been a wife-sale at 'Casterbridge' at that time. The main part of the action falls between 1846 and 1849, the critical years of the repeal of the Corn Laws.

In the time-scale *The Mayor* follows immediately after *The Return of the Native,* whose action belongs to the years 1842-3. For the 1850s and 1860s we have *Jude the Obscure,* and *Two on a Tower,* and for the early 1870s *Far from the Madding Crowd,* one of Hardy's most satisfying stories. It began to appear as a serial in *The Cornhill Magazine* in January 1874, which makes the time of the events of the tale almost contemporary. From internal evidence, particularly the description of Bathsheba's farmhouse at the opening of Chapter 9, it is possible to judge that we are at a time of agricultural — or at least 'landlord' — depression, which suggests the 'Bad Seventies' following upon the great age of High Farming of early Victorian England. Bathsheba, a working farmeress, occupies

> a hoary building, of the early stage of Classic Renaissance as regards its architecture, and of a proportion which told at a glance that, as is so frequently the case, it had once been the manorial hall upon a small estate around it, now altogether effaced as a distinct property, and merged in the vast tract of a non-residential landlord, which comprised several such modest demesnes.

It had (and has, as may be seen from a glance at its original, Waterston House, near Puddletown) fluted pilasters, panelled or columnar chimneys, and coped gables with finials. And Hardy tells us that

> the whole prospect here . . . suggested to the imagination that on the adaptation of the building for farming purposes the vital principle of the house had turned round inside its body to face the other way. Reversals of this kind, strange deformities, tremendous paralyses, are often

seen to be inflicted by trade upon edifices . . . which were originally planned for pleasure alone.

It was a building, to employ a rather misleading expression, that had 'come down in the world' — that is, from a home of the squirearchy to the headquarters of a working farm. It is the kind of social change that Hardy would readily understand, though he makes no fuss about it. To have understood it might have saved a great deal of puzzlement, and some ill-informed criticism, among those who have seen the film of the novel and expressed surprise at Bathsheba's living behind a facade of Renaissance architecture — living 'above her station'. What have been called 'the Bad Seventies' were not on the whole bad for the Bathsheba Everdenes.

The Woodlanders belongs to a later part of the seventies, but the date seems unimportant on account of the secluded and unchanging character of Little Hintock, 'one of those sequestered spots outside the gates of the world where may usually be found more meditation than action . . .' Here the apple-trees of old South's orchard recorded in their crippled slant to the north-east the great November gale of 1824. Here Mr George Melbury, 'timber, bark and copse-ware merchant', lived in a house which was of 'respectable, roomy, almost dignified aspect' and which suggested that Little Hintock had once been of greater importance. The house looked at you 'from the still distinct middle- distance of the early Georgian time'. Here, itinerant barbers might buy the beautiful hair of country-girls like Marty South to sell to local ladies of uncertain age like Mrs Charmond who lived, like many another lonely lady of her kind, in damp old country houses outside the village. *The Woodlanders* was published in 1886-7, and relates to the years 1876-9, though its setting in a sylvan region that Hardy had not yet brought within the scope of his 'exhibition of Wessex life' and of which he was inordinately fond is more important than the temporal dating of its action or its social portraiture. *A Laodicean,* which was published in 1881, some five years earlier than *The Woodlanders,* is actually sub-titled 'A Story of Today', and *Tess of the d'Urbervilles,* published in 1891, has an action which takes place at the end of the 1880s. Hardy's only avowed 'historical novel', *The Trumpet-Major,* takes the reader back to the first decade of the nineteenth century, but for all its carefully assembled paraphernalia of the costume novel it is somehow less impressive as a historical document than most of the others.

The fact is that when Hardy wrote of the world he knew, the world he had lived in, the English countryside in the half-century between the repeal of the Corn Laws and the tragedy of Tess, a Wessex which was 'slipping out of his fingers, changing shape beyond what he remembered from his youth, receding into history', he was putting on record a history which he had lived on his pulses, and, for that very reason, it was a history more real than anything he could turn out in a 'historical novel' properly so called. How far was he aware of this? He was certainly well enough aware that his novels recorded the graveward descent of a civilisation or of an ancient way of life, although that was not why he wrote them. He rarely spoke, or wrote, didactically of what was happening, and least of all did he sing swan-songs. For one thing he never suffered from the delusion that 'things are not what they used to be', largely because he knew in his shrewd old country-dweller's way that they never are. Nor did he idealise a way that was departing. He came from a stratum of society which has always lived close to poverty and loss, suffering and rough weather, a part of society that has never had much time for the luxury of lamentation or the pleasures of nostalgia. The poet who wrote 'A Trampwoman's Tragedy' and 'Weathers' was no melancholy elegist. He was like the shepherd who is not content to grizzle about bad weather but shuns it. We should have been spared a great deal of nonsense about Hardy's pessimism if critics had deigned to notice that the victims in his novels are generally people who have lacked the foresight or the good sense to forfend the consequences of their own folly. Even the tragedy of Tess is in no small part brought about by the feckless, even senseless, character of her family. Not for nothing did Hardy belong to an England which bought thousands of copies of the *Self-help* of Samuel Smiles. *Jude the Obscure* is a failure in part because its author does not allow his 'poor puppet' even the rudiments of good fortune which the reader knows would have come his way in real life and because Jude never omits an opportunity to dwell upon the consequences of his own weakness for the occasional bout of lechery and strong liquor.

There is no fuss or foolishness about 'the good old days' in Hardy's picture of the changing world. He left it to his critics in the twentieth century to indulge in jargon about the decline of the 'organic community' and its replacement by a situation which D.H. Lawrence was to name 'anti-life'. Hardy's essay of 1883 on 'The Dorsetshire Labourer' ought to be reprinted in sufficient quantities to present a copy to every sociologist, or sociological literary critic, in England and America. Talking of the increased migration of the labourer and his family he finds little cause for lamentation. The annual removal was to be regarded as 'the most natural thing in the world', and in the younger families 'a pleasant excitement'. Many advantages accrued to the labourer from the varied experience it brought. It made the labourers shrewder and sharper men of the world, teaching them to hold their own with firmness and judgement. It was no doubt true that they tended to lose their peculiarities as a class:

> That seclusion and immutability, which was so bad for their pockets, was an unrivalled fosterer of their personal charm in the eyes of those whose experiences had been less limited. But the artistic merit of their old condition is scarcely a reason why they should have continued in it when other communities were marching on so vigorously towards uniformity and mental equality. It is only the old story that progress and picturesqueness do not harmonise. They are losing their individuality, but they are widening the range of their ideas, and gaining in freedom. It is too much to expect them to remain stagnant and old fashioned for the pleasure of romantic spectators.[2]

While their pecuniary condition was bettered by these changes and their freedom enlarged, Hardy concedes that 'they have lost touch with their environment, and that sense of long local participancy which is one of the pleasures of age'. Yet, on the other hand, he protests that 'new varieties of happiness evolve themselves like new varieties of plants', and that 'new charms may have arisen among the classes who have been driven to adopt the remedy of locomotion for evils of oppression and poverty . . .' Hardy appreciated as well as anyone the value in terms of human kindness and protection of the ancient personal relationship between lord and man, but he valued still more the freedom and independence, the enhancement of human dignity, that were being brought about by the 'increasing nomadic habit of the labourer'. He was a philosophical Radical of Joseph Arch's England.

The range of Hardy's historical reference is very wide, but its quality is extremely uneven. This is as it should be. He read history as any educated man read it in Victorian England. Thucydides, Clarendon, Gibbon, Motley, were all in his library, and all were cherished. By reason of his two professions, architecture and novel-writing, certain periods and certain aspects of history claimed his attention much more than others. The Middle Ages absorbed him simply and solely because they produced the best, or the most familiar, building. Georgian England, of course, was the age and the place of the best local history (except the Roman) as Weymouth and Bath make abundantly clear. And there were, as ever, family connections: 'the mention of the Duke of Monmouth was likely to set T.H. talking', says Edmund Blunden, for he believed that his ancestors had assisted the Duke's escape after Sedgemoor (the 'sad Sedge-Moor' of 'A Trampwoman's Tragedy'), and he wrote one of his short stories about this incident and called it 'The Duke's Reappearance'. One of his later stories, 'A Committee-Man of "The Terror" ' (1896) is located among 'the Georgian glories of our old-fashioned watering-place', and recreates the detail of George III at Weymouth almost precisely in the terms of *The Trumpet-Major* of sixteen years before. Some of the short stories are little more than sweepings of the workshop that produced the novels and *The Dynasts*. 'A Tradition of Eighteen Hundred and Four', 'The Melancholy Hussar' and 'Enter a Dragoon' are all notable examples.

Hardy's fascination by the local connection with old Rome may be seen in his short story, 'A Tryst at an Ancient Earthwork', and everyone knows the famous evocation of the legions in *The Mayor of Casterbridge:*

Casterbridge announced old Rome in every street, alley and precinct. It looked Roman, bespoke the art of Rome, concealed dead men of Rome. It was impossible to dig more than a foot or two deep about the town fields and gardens without coming upon some tall soldier or other of the Empire, who had lain there in his silent unobtrusive rest for a space of fifteen hundred years.[3]

There is fond exaggeration here, doubtless, but no one with the slightest historical imagination can ever regret the sunshine vision of the legion in the Amphitheatre:

... some old people said that at certain moments in the summer time, in broad daylight, persons sitting with a book or dozing in the arena had, on lifting their eyes, beheld the slopes lined with a gazing legion of Hadrian's soldiery as if watching the gladiatorial combat; and had heard the roar of their excited voices...[4]

The same evocation is established in 'A Tryst at an Ancient Earthwork' (which is obviously Maiden Castle, near Dorchester) where the play of lightning over the slopes of the earthwork,

bears a fanciful resemblance to swords moving in combat ... Men must often have gone out by those gates in the morning to battle with the Roman legions under Vespasian.... We can almost hear the stream of years that have borne these deeds away from us. Strange articulations seem to float on the air ... There arises an ineradicable fancy that they are human voices ... lingering air-borne vibrations of conversations uttered at least fifteen hundred years ago.[5]

Here men have celebrated daring, strength, cruelty, everything except 'simple loving-kindness'. That was the element in history that Hardy found lacking, that and the praise, even the recording, of the creative endeavours of anonymous men. He will have us recall at Maiden Castle the 'remote mind' which had once said, 'Let it be built here!' Who was that man?

Whether he were some great one of the Belgae, or of the

Durotriges, or the travelling engineer of Britain's united
tribes, must for ever remain time's secret; his form cannot
be realized, nor his countenance, nor the tongue that he
spoke, when he set down his foot with a thud and said,
'Let it be here!'[6]

Perhaps the best-known of Hardy's attempts to memorialise
such forgotten men is in his poem, 'The Abbey Mason',
which sought to celebrate the unknown 'inventor of the
"Perpendicular" style of Gothic Architecture'. This unsung
hero, he tells us, learnt his art from the patterns left upon his
'chalk-scratched' drawing-board by the frost and rain:

> 'Surely the hand of God it is
> That conjured so, and only His! —

> 'Disclosing by the frost and rain
> Forms your invention chased in vain;

says the abbot, denying the Abbey Mason his chance of fame.
It remains for Abbot Horton in the poem, years later, to
point out that the Abbey Mason

> '. . . did but what all artists do,
> Wait upon Nature for his cue'.

but by then it was too late and the architect's name had been
forgotten. Hardy could not resist the irony of the fact that

> . . . some minds so modest be
> As to renounce fame's fairest fee, . . .

> While others boom a baseless claim,
> And upon nothing rear a name.

'The Abbey Mason' bears at its head a reference to his
memories of his old master in the art of architecture, John
Hicks of Dorchester.

Hardy's archaeological interests are borne out at the
Dorchester Museum and in a number of contributions to
archaeological journals. He built his house close to a notable
barrow, Conquer Barrow, near Dorchester, and in 1890 wrote
a paper giving an account of Romano-British urns and
skeletons discovered in digging the foundations. If he had not
become a working novelist he could well have well lived his

life as a professional architect, just as he might have become a
classical scholar or an archaeologist. 'What a biographer was
lost when nature stamped Novelist on your brow!'[7] Edmund
Gosse exclaimed after reading Hardy's obituary of William
Barnes with its fine description of that aged clergyman
trudging up the narrow South Street of Dorchester every
Saturday morning.[8] The one art that may safely be declared
outside his scope, however, is that of the historian. Like Carlyle
he was too much under the dominion of the two things
which must ever be the historian's greatest enemies: passion
and philosophy. Philosophy has ruined more possible
historians than any other vice. The historian must be wedded
to the particular, whereas the philosopher, like the poet,
deals in universals. Similarly, the historian must eschew
passion, and if he possesses much of it he had better turn to
poetry: not to fiction, which is often more 'true' than either
history or nature can be. 'Passion' is the only name for that
exaltation which bears a man above the commonplace, the
judicious, the careful balancing of opposites. It is not a name
for excess or absence of control. Hardy had both the concern
with universals and the *afflatus* of the poet, and between the
two he was, again like Carlyle, incapable of keeping his eyes
closed sufficiently to the heights or the depths of human
experience for the fulfilment of the historian's subaltern
tasks.

2 The Pattern in the Carpet

Temperamentally, then, Thomas Hardy was ill-equipped to write history. History is concerned with mutation, and Hardy, a poet first and last, was concerned with the immutable. All the same, at the age of fifty, he recorded his conviction that 'persons are successively various persons, according as each special strand in their characters is brought uppermost by circumstances',[1] an observation that few novelists would trouble to write down after living for half a century. Moreover, it is an observation that this particular practitioner of the craft of fiction consistently ignored when he set pen to paper in pursuit of his livelihood. *A propos* of the bowdlerisation of *The Mayor of Casterbridge* for serial publication in *The Graphic* he remarked that 'after all, it is not improbabilities of incident but improbabilities of character that matter',[2] and probability of character to Hardy meant consistency. It meant that his own characters, while they might behave with sufficient human craziness to help their author weave his plot, would always be the same persons over the course of the story. With one or two exceptions, such as Bathsheba Everdene, Hardy's characters do not change, or grow, or even learn very much as they pursue their ill-starred adventures. They are not 'successively various persons', but children of unconscious propensity. The mark of their doom is on their foreheads from the beginning. It might be said, indeed, that they suffer because they cannot change.

The singularity of Thomas Hardy, and the greater part of his genius, spring from the fact that he showed that same fixity of character which he imparts to the creatures of his imagination. It has been said of his work that it shows a lack of development, that there is no essential difference between the best of his early and the best of his later work. The point is one of criticism, and might easily be justified by an examination of his technique at various stages of his career as a man of letters. 'Early Hardy', 'Middle Hardy' and 'Late Hardy' do not exist as valid terms of differential description. At the very most it might be said that one could 'place' a Hardy novel or poem by reason of the emphasis laid upon certain imported 'ideas', but even this could not be attempted with complete confidence. There are glimpses of 'The New Woman' in *Far from the Madding Crowd* (1874), in *A Laodicean* (1881), as well as in *Jude the Obscure* (1895), and no doubt if we possessed *The Poor Man and the Lady*, his first, unpublished, novel, we should find in it even more of the 'social criticism' that we find in his last major work of fiction. The truth is that in one sense Hardy developed remarkably early, and in another more important sense he never developed at all. He knew most of what he wanted to say about life as certainly at five-and-twenty as he knew half a century later. All that really happened in the long course of his literary life was that the English public became less unwilling to 'take it'. As he remarked in 1889, 'truth to character is not considered quite such a crime in literature as it was formerly',[3] although he was yet to experience the recalcitrance of the public towards *Tess* and *Jude*. Hardy was prepared to speak out in Aeschylean grimness in Victorian England, but he toned down his darker shades until the century was near its close. A great artist, as Coleridge observed, has to create the taste by which his best work is judged. Perhaps the process was never completed in Hardy's lifetime.

There is a sense in which the great imaginative artist never learns anything. 'Will the world never learn', George Moore once asked in pardonable exasperation, 'that we never learn anything that we did not know before?' He meant very much what Hardy meant when he spoke of the artist following his own pattern in the carpet.

As, in looking at a carpet, by following one colour a certain pattern is suggested, by following another colour, another; so in life the seer should watch that pattern among general things which his idiosyncrasy moves him to observe, and describe that alone. This is, quite accurately, a going to Nature; yet the result is no mere photograph, but purely the product of the writer's own mind.[4]

In looking at life, the seer — and to Hardy the great imaginative writer, more especially the poet, was ever a seer, no less — will 'bring out the features which illustrate the author's idiosyncratic mode of regard'. That mode is the product of his peculiar temperament, and he selects his material habitually in accordance with its character and quality. Hardy knew from the beginning, just as the great artist may be said to know the laws of his own being without, or before, formulating them. It was negatively expressed in a note which he had made as a young man of twenty-five struggling to realise his potentialities in London:

> More conducive to success in life than the desire for much knowledge is the being satisfied with ignorance on irrelevant subjects.[5]

This economy of effort is achieved by an unerring and intuitive apprehension of the essential. The mind and spirit of the imaginative genius, as Professor Livingston Lowes showed in *The Road to Xanadu* finds its own food and rejects all else but that. It finds what is required in order to nourish its own peculiar nature, as certain birds feed exclusively on certain berries and leave others, seemingly no less attractive, strictly alone. In the case of the poet or novelist, we may say, the individual's 'idiosyncratic mode of regard'[6] will determine that it makes use of certain subjects and rejects all others. The novelist will tell only his own kind of stories. We are told that Guy de Maupassant offered to pay ƒ.100 to anyone that sent him an anecdote he could use. The operative word here is 'could'. These are the stories, or the poems, that come — as D. H. Lawrence put it — 'unwatched from the pen' — as distinct from the doctrine which is fabricated from the wholly conscious intelligence. These are the works that modify men's souls in the reading like an experience of life itself, the necessary fruits of an 'idiosyncratic mode of regard', the mysterious fruits of a temperament.

The temperament of Hardy, the peculiar organisation of

his moral and emotional being which evinces itself everywhere unchanged and unchanging throughout his work, was
the offspring of a civilisation which was dying when he was
born and which is now as extinct, as truly 'historical', as that
of Knossos or Herculaneum, and the significance of his work
is only to be apprehended by an effort of historical
reconstruction. Purely literary, or aesthetic, criticism has said
much, and may yet say more. What we want to know about
Hardy by this time is something other than literary criticism
can provide. We want to know why, despite all his obvious
defects as a writer, his awkwardnesses of style, his painful
efforts to be 'literary', his creaking plots and quadrille-like
appositions of character, his pedantic art references and
scientific jargon, he yet has been, and still remains, so great a
force in the emotional lives of men and women who see, and
yet do not worry about, these defects. Men and women who
bring to their reading a wide and cultivated background of
intellectual and emotional experience read these works with a
persistency born not of fortitude but love. Sir Llewellyn
Woodward, the distinguished historian, tells us that he found
in Thomas Hardy the greatest single influence in his early
years at Oxford, and that he went on to make the novels and
poems a part of his own life by constant reading and
rereading over the years that followed. A multitude of
persons of intellectual eminence could lay their hands on
their hearts and say the same. Of course there are certain
undergraduates of youthful and of advancing years who will
say things like, 'I should never have known Hardy was a great
novelist unless I had been told so', or (in a later jargon)
'Hardy, of course, is out'. Yet even the ignorant who would
place Hardy low in the scale of English do not find it easy to
ignore him and his tremendous success and lasting popularity.
Even the condescending Henry James, who called him 'the
good little Thomas Hardy', would have understood that the
indigenous culture of the England he loved so well flowered
from a morality whose roots lay at Stratford, Ottery St Mary,
Cockermouth and a thousand small country towns and
villages like Higher Bockhampton. Generation after generation the men and women of this ancient soil had met life and
death in the presence of the immensities of sky and sea, moor

and hill. Myths had descended upon them from pulpit and altar, and they had employed their symbolism as a vestment, rough and often ill-fitting, for the deepest feelings engendered in their hearts by their experience of human destiny upon the earth. They made songs and dances, tales and mumming-plays, to shadow forth an ancestral wisdom. Living hard by nature and its unchanging rhythm and its senseless horseplay, they came to a grave irony and a monumental patience. Their most cherished virtue was endurance, their most abhorred sin was breach of faith between man and man in face of the everlasting enemy — earth and the elements and fate. They knew nothing of 'Art' but everything of life: the life which persists beneath and beyond the little luxuries of Christian piety and consolation. Generations who knew not Adam have collected and appraised the work of their hands and named it 'Folk', but the folk themselves called it quite other names — pots and pans, butts and byres, bartons and cottages, 'The New-Rigged Ship' and 'The Western Tragedy' and 'Haste to the Wedding'. In the fullness of time they sent a chosen child to the High School and the University College in Nottingham, a man-child who gave utterance to the life of his fathers in the immortal opening of a novel called *The Rainbow*. Another went to school at Dorchester and later to evening-classes at King's College, London.

'He was', said a Cambridge don who had spent an afternoon with the old man on the occasion of his installation as an Honorary Fellow of Magdalene College, 'a strange mixture of an old countryman and a pass degree man. . . he talked chiefly about a favourite dog; he wanted to see the Second Court of St. John's because Ruskin said . . .' This was ancient Wessex absorbing 'culture'; the articulate representative of a culture older and deeper than that of the University Schools, modestly exploring a world which had moved on from the world of Egdon Heath, the Great Plain, and the Vale of Blackmore. It was as if in him the dwellers in these solitary places had gathered together the near-spent forces of their ancient life in order to utter a strange, half-articulate cry before the tide of a later age should submerge them for ever. Thomas Hardy went far beyond such a commission. He uttered much else than the voice of his own people. Nor would they have recognised in his utterance their own largely unconscious philosophy, for to them it was not philosophy but plain commonsense, the unspoken wisdom of hard-driven men and women who have a day's work to do between dawn and sunset. But what he thought and felt and said was near enough to what they thought and felt and would have said if — strangest of imaginings — they had become the clever, book-learned, vocal young Hardy who went to school at Dorchester and later trained as an architect and went to Mr Blomfield's office in London.

Thus it was to be all his life: the boy reading Cassell's *Popular Educator* on the edge of Egdon; the young man in London attending French classes at King's College, resting his copy of Shakespeare on the orchestra-rail at Drury Lane while Phelps played Richard III; spending twenty minutes every lunch-hour at the National Gallery and 'confining his attention to a single master on each visit, and forbidding his eyes to stray to any other';[7] the successful novelist musing among the antiquities of the British Museum and working his way industriously through Hegel and Schopenhauer in the Reading Room; filling scores of notebooks with the neat, sensitive hand of the scholar; returning again and again in his old age to his shabby shilling editions of Shelley, Wordsworth and Keats; browsing almost daily upon his favourite Greek and Latin authors; carefully copying out his latest lyric for a London editor, and seldom failing to enclose a stamped addressed envelope for its quite incredible return. Max Beerbohm tells a story of Hardy's sending a poem to the newly-founded *London Mercury* and saying, 'Ah, these young men, they're very kind — they took it'. Hardy was then eighty and one of England's most famous poets.

And yet, this 'culture', what did it amount to after all? 'It doesn't help much', he wrote after a careful course of Hegel on the Real and Rational in 1886. 'These venerable philosophers seem to start wrong; they cannot get away from a prepossession that the world must somehow have been made to be a comfortable place for man.'[8] Men knew better than that in Wessex. He was sardonically amused to hear Middleton, Slade Professor of Fine Art at Cambridge, talk of bishops' copes and mitres in an earnest, serious, anxious manner, as if there were no cakes and ale in the world, nor laughter and tears, nor misery beyond tears. Such people had no sense of life as such. Their concern with 'art' had caused them to lose all sense of art's subsidiary relation to existence. And there was Henry James. 'James's subjects are those one could be interested in at moments when there is nothing larger to think of',[9] thought Hardy. He noted, too, that: 'The literary productions of men of rigidly good family and rigidly correct education, mostly treat social conventions . . . as if they were cardinal facts of life.'[10] They were all so much concerned with the mere vesture, or appearances, of things, and they were all so like dear Matthew Arnold who 'had a manner of having made up his mind upon everything years ago'. Some little time before he read any Henry James, Hardy had discovered that he was 'living in a world where nothing bears out in practice what it promises incipiently'. Since that time, he observed, 'I have troubled myself very little about theories . . . Where development according to perfect reason is limited to the narrow region of pure mathematics, I am content with tentativeness from day to day.'[11]

Thus 'culture', painfully acquired, shrank to a husk or shell upon the flesh of the living man who knew what men and women make of life in the daily living of it. Thomas Hardy was no peasant. He prized what men had won for themselves by the stress of hard thinking and deep feeling. He especially respected scholarship, and he loved learning. His roots ran deep into an ancient society which had never lost touch with its intellectual ancestry. His temperament had the immutable quality of the folk of the fields who wear neither spectacles nor blinkers, yet he grew up to employ the lingo of a pseudo-scientific age. Living between two worlds, the rural world of his fathers and the up-and-coming world of the universal bourgeoisie, he uttered the last judgement of his kind upon the dilemma of modern man. For it was the dilemma of Thomas Hardy. He, too, had outgrown the myth of Eden, the prepossession that the world must somehow have been intended to be a comfortable place for men. It was a prepossession that ancient Wessex had never possessed, but there was a time when the young Hardy for a brief moment

succumbed to it. The moment soon passed. 'Had the
teachings of experience grown cumulatively with the age of
the world', he noted when he was twenty-seven, 'we should
have been ere now as great as God.'[12] But they hadn't, and we
weren't, and Hardy had known it all the time in his heart. He
went on saying so for the rest of his life.

At the head of his last major work of fiction Hardy wrote
the words, THE LETTER KILLETH. The phrase might fitly
stand at the head of any essay on Hardy as a man of letters,
for the utterance of all that lay behind his unique temperament was unlikely ever to find itself effectively expressed in
any of the established forms of literature. In the end he was
obscurely aware of this. What he sought to achieve in *The
Dynasts* was a vast shadow-show of destiny, a complex of
song and dance and mime which should project into the mind
of the reader the realities which lie behind appearance.

> My art is to intensify the expression of things . . . so that
> the heart and inner meaning is made vividly visible . . . The
> realities to be the true realities of life, hitherto called
> abstractions. The old material realities to be placed behind
> the former, as shadowy accessories.[13]

What interested him, what his idiosyncratic mode of regard or
his peculiar temperament led him to see, was the inner
meaning of things, for he was first and last a seer into things
rather than an expert rapporteur of their external aspect. He
was a Realist only in the sense that medieval Schoolmen
employed that name to dissociate themselves from Nomina-
lists, or as the term is used of Plato and the Platonists, for
whom only the Ideas were real. When in 1897 he published
The Pursuit of the Well-Beloved in volume form simply as
The Well-Beloved, he confessed that it had been sketched
'when I was comparatively a young man, and interested in
the Platonic Idea, which, considering its charm and its
poetry, one could well wish to be interested in always'.[14] He
was all his life a reader of Greek and familiar with what his
idol, Shelley, called 'Plato's gorgeous nonsense'. He noted
down the germinal idea of *The Well-Beloved* only a fortnight
after recording his reading of Plato's dialogue, *Cratylus,* in
1889.

A very good way of looking at things would be to regard
everything as having an actual or false name, and an
intrinsic or true name, to ascertain which all endeavour
would be made . . . The fact is that nearly all things are
falsely, or rather inadequately, named.[15]

It is important that the novels should be read in the light
of this conception of *The Dynasts,* in other words we should
go backwards from the poetry to the prose. Otherwise we
shall continue to waste time in comparing Hardy with George
Eliot. We have to bring ourselves to see Tess Durbeyfield not
as a Dorset milkmaid who 'got into trouble', and Jude
Fawley not as a local lad who 'couldn't go to Oxford'; we
have to see that they belong to a different dimension from
that of Hetty Sorrel and Felix Holt; that they have rather the
epic quality of figures in *Everyman, The Pilgrim's Progress,
Paradise Lost* and *The Tempest.* The greatest figures of the
world's imaginings transcend the limits of the personal and are
clothed in abstraction. Only when we understand this shall
we cease to judge them as 'real' or 'true to life' or otherwise.
We may even cease to discourse on 'the static nature of
Hardy's characterisation', or 'the rigid and diagrammatic
structure of his plots', or 'his incredible use of coincidence'.
We shall indeed begin to appraise Hardy in terms of his
intention. If we regret that he did not continue to write
novels in the vein of *Under the Greenwood Tree,* which he
himself sub-titled 'A Rural Painting of the Dutch School', let
us recall that in his middle forties he was already tired of
looking at the Bonington which hung in the drawing-room at
Max Gate.

I don't want to see landscapes, i.e. scenic paintings of them
[he wrote in his journal] because I don't want to see the
original realities — as optical effects, that is. I want to see
the deeper reality underlying the scenic, the expression of
what are sometimes called the abstract imaginings. The
'simply natural' is interesting no longer. The much decried,
mad, late-Turner rendering is now necessary to create my
interest. The exact truth as to material fact ceases to be of
importance in art — it is a student's style — the style of a
period when the mind is serene and unawakened to the

tragical mysteries of life; when it does not bring anything
to the object that coalesces with and translates the
qualities that are already there, — half hidden, it may be —
and the two united are depicted as the All.[16]

It has often been imagined that Hardy failed to grasp the
true significance of his work. Rebecca West once said that in
his briefer compositions 'there obtruded on him his habitual
perplexity as to what art could possibly be about,' although
it is true that she also allowed that when he became engaged
on a long and important book 'his lack of comprehension of
what art was about mattered nothing' because, like other
artists, he fell into the equivalent of a trance state and the
unconscious did the rest. Thanks to Florence Hardy's *The
Life of Thomas Hardy* which we now know was, of course,
written mostly by Hardy himself, and the important and
valuable compilations from the notebooks and papers which
it contains, we are in a position to assert that Hardy knew a
great deal more of the workings of his own genius than a
study of the corpus of his work, with its failures of complete
self-realisation, would lead one to suppose, and certainly a
vast deal more than the generality of his critics. It remains
true, however, that to the end of his long life he never set
down any clearly articulated statement of his intention. Just
as in politics, so in literature, he never enlisted in any form of
sports-club, although he made regular notes for the more
profitable pursuit of his trade. However, the relations which
subsisted between his temperament and the products of his
pen, and more especially the integral relations which subsisted between Thomas Hardy, the Eminent Man of Letters,
and the historic culture of the old English society from which
he sprang, only seemed to flash upon him piecemeal and in
fleeting moments, rarely in full consciousness. He knew, for
instance, that he chose his themes because of his personal
idiosyncrasy, or his 'idiosyncratic mode of regard'. He always
hated people to talk about 'Thomas Hardy's philosophy',
denying that he ever intended to do more than 'give shape
and coherence to a series of seemings, or personal impres-
sions'. He knew perfectly well that the notion of a man's
philosophy and experience of life colouring his art is an easy
assumption of the literary critic, and that to talk of Thomas

Hardy trying, consciously or otherwise to embody his philosophical reactions in literary form is a type of literary gibberish. Even D.H. Lawrence wrote of his 'subduing his art to a metaphysic', though he came to see later that the artistic form preceded and directed the metaphysic. Few critics ever seem to see that a novelist's so-called philosophy is mostly a technical device for telling the sort of story he wants to tell, and that his choice of his peculiar fable is determined by the idiosyncratic mode of regard which directs his vision to one particular pattern in the carpet, or that the temperament which in turn decides this is probably the consequence of physical or even genetic factors. What precisely that temperament was in Thomas Hardy some attempt must be made to ascertain.

3   The Birth of a Temperament

Hardy's temperament was that of his kind, the offspring of the society that produced him. It was complete before he was twenty years old, and it never changed. It is the fixed and consistent character of a deeply inbred type, as fixed and consistent as the character of the people in his books.

Of course, it is always dangerous to say that a man was *born* this, or that, but one is greatly tempted to say it of Hardy, the more so because he would doubtless have said it himself. He believed firmly in the profound importance of heredity, a fact which brings us at once to the countryman. Among the dwellers in remote places, the lonely villages of old England, notions of hereditary powers and qualities were most carefully cherished. When men live their lives in the daily presence of continuity — the unchanging hills, the unvarying rhythm of the seasons, the ancient memorials of the churchyard, the fireside talk of old men and women who mumble their memories like living calendars of births, marriages and deaths, they come to refer habitually to the warranty of birth and ancestry. Hardy grew up with the unfolding of the generations ever in his ears, and he acquired the concern for heredity which is characteristic of his kind and which we find as an important element in some of the novels and in such poems as 'Heredity' and 'Night in the Old Home'. All his life he was gathering and brooding upon scraps of local lore about the mingled generations of Hardys, Swetmans, Childs and Hands who had lived for centuries in the Vale of Blackmore and the valley of the Frome.

This, his concern for the heredity of the Hardys, was tinged with a certain pride, and with a certain regret for the fading of past glories. His forebears had played no mean part in the making of the society they inhabited, and there was in Hardy, as Edmund Blunden has observed, 'a strain of resentment, as of one excluded, unplaced . . . a reticent pride, as of one with a lineage'. The Hardys were an ancient family in decline. Thomas believed them to descend from one Clement le Hardy, Lieutenant-Governor of Jersey in the later fifteenth century, and at one time he seriously considered reimporting the ancestral 'le' into his patronymic — 'Thomas le Hardy'. It had a 'county' sound; and the eminent novelist, with his countryman's build and colouring, was not infrequently made aware of his lack of the outward marks of 'county' breeding. Perhaps the first Mrs Hardy had something to do with it, being intimately connected with 'the higher order of the clergy'. Possibly she made 'the good little Thomas Hardy', son of a small builder and life-renter at Higher Bockhampton, feel that a little parading of the Hardy pedigree would not be out of place, especially when the eminent novelist and his lady came to mix in County and London society.

With Thomas, however, the thing had little or nothing to do with the mean surface of social snobbery. He had reason enough to regret the purely material decline that had overtaken the family: the loss of solid acres and of hard cash. It was a calamity that had afflicted both the Hardys and his mother's family, the Swetmans, and it appears to have been nobody's fault but their own — a matter of personal improvidence and unfortunate marriages. Thomas Hardy could and did lament this whenever he saw some decayed member of his clan driving a shabby horse and cart, or whenever he surveyed some scene of former family proprietage. 'The decline and fall of the Hardys much in evidence here-about', he notes on a visit in 1888 to Woolcombe, once a Hardy property. 'So we go down, down, down.'[1] But his concern went deeper still. It was not so much a question whether the Hardys had ever been 'county'. It was rather a question of character, of vitality, or virtue. Hardy saw his own family with its declining fortunes as a sign and symptom of the end of a culture, and in 'Night in the Old Home', the poem in which he imagines himself as talking to his 'ancestors, he describes himself as 'A pale late plant of your once strong stock'.

Time and again, Hardy would discourse upon this, his

favourite topic in the history of Wessex. It occurs again and
again in his work as poet and novelist. Talking to a visiting
journalist at Max Gate, he would speak of his people with
nostalgic pride. They bore the features, many of these rustic
labourers, of the portraits in the old manor-houses. He
himself possessed the pedigree of the Durbeyfields right back
to the Conquest. These people were, they must be, he would
assert, descendants of the Romans who had lived here for
centuries and whose relics lay everywhere beneath the land
they tilled —'They are the representatives of antiquity'. But
most of all they had the character of an ancient people, a
unique character, quite distinct from that of our latter-day
urban mob:

> There is a certain conscious pride about some of these
> people, which differentiates them at once from middle-
> class cockneyism or provincialism . . . They are full of
> character, which is not to be found in the strained,
> calculating, unromantic middle classes.[2]

This character was the offspring of antiquity, of the self-
identification of an ancient people; unique and constant in
the flux of generations. To possess this character, to cherish
it, to live by it, and to look upon all life through its single
vision: this, not the recovery of ancestral acres, was the pride
of the singularly modest man who now spoke its austere and
ancient message to a world that was passing onwards to
another mode of life. It was for this that he was proud of
what Wessex had done in the world, and, in particular, what
had been done by the Hardys. He had the portrait of his
kinsman, Nelson's great flag-captain, opposite his own in the
drawing-room at Max Gate. Max Gate, designed by himself,
was itself a monument to what a Hardy could still achieve
'far from the madding crowd'. He himself designed the Latin
inscription in Stinsford Church to the three generations of
the Hardys who had made music in the gallery there. His own
body, in the end, was to be cremated and the ashes to lie in
London, but his heart was to be buried in Stinsford
churchyard among the 'local hearts and heads'.

The temperament which bloomed from this old stock was
at once simple and profound. Its simplicity shows itself both

in externals — the habit of the man as the world saw him in the flesh and habiliments of daily life — and in the instinctive standards by which he lived and worked. In appearance, gait and manner he was unaffectedly vulgar, employing that word in its original and noble meaning of common, as distinct from esoteric. 'A somewhat fair-complexioned man, a trifle below the middle-height, of slight build, with a pleasant thoughtful face, exceptionally broad at the temples, and fringed by a beard trimmed after the Elizabethan manner.' Spare, but not thin, trim at the shoulders, with long deft fingers and a light easy gait. A rapid walker. Alert, with grey, observant eyes. A man whose clothes one would never notice, except that his trousers tended to bag at the knee and his coat-sleeves to hang a little far over his wrists. The kind of man one would not notice in a crowd, except that one might wonder sometimes whether he were not quietly making notes like the 'chiel' in Burns. He always wore a hard collar, and he carried his hat — a straw-yard in summer, and ordinary felt in winter or when he was in London — square on his head: never at the least bit of an angle. A raincoat folded on his arm, an unfurled umbrella, good country boots, and — late in life — not an Elizabethan beard but a straggling moustache. This was the man who, in the year of grace 1870 counted out £75 in Bank of England notes on his publisher's desk as his share of the risk of publishing *Desperate Remedies,* much to that gentleman's astonishment, and who never missed a circus, a travelling show or a set of lancers in his life if he could help it. He liked dancing, cycling, fiddling, singing glees, and he cared little for alcohol and not at all for tobacco. In his private journal he refers to his intended wife as 'Miss G' after knowing her for nearly three years, and to the end of his life he refused to be weighed because he held it to be unlucky.

With his unaffected demeanour and simplicity of tastes went an unquestionable integrity of character. The goodness of 'the good little Thomas Hardy' was somehow the precious counterpart of his homespun externals. He had the integrity of the land and the people who bred him: the straight-cut love of 'making a good job' of whatever he might undertake. It is quite inconceivable that Hardy should ever have shown the faintest trace of carelessness in execution, whether he were drawing a church, designing a memorial or composing a lyric. Mrs Hardy in the *Life* tells the reader of 'Hardy's artistic inability to rest content with anything that he wrote until he had brought the expression as near to his thought as language would allow.'[3] His handwriting speaks the whole truth of the man with its neat but flowing characters, its clear and graceful masculinity. It is the hand of a scholar-artist, and indeed there is much of the scholar — the man of grave and industrious purpose — throughout all his career and work. He 'made notes', he visited his scenes before he wrote, he expended infinite care upon the detailed accuracy of fact whenever fact was called for. His work is designed, four-square, with carefully laid foundations, like the work he did in his first profession as architect. True, he sometimes appears to disparage his own work but we should not be misled, as some minor critics have been, by this mixture of modesty and whimsical humour. In opening a Hardy novel, the reader feels at once that a craftsman is in charge. The author inspires confidence in his ability to carry the thing through. Generations of country craftsmen, the men who cut the dykes, tilled the waste, and built the mills and churches and cottages and manor-houses, stand behind this sound contriving. It is all a little out of fashion; but then, so are the mills and churches. Like them, it will endure.

Turning inwards from these outward marks of simple honesty, we find first and foremost a simple honesty of vision. This is the thing about Hardy that most disconcerts the world of make-believe in which the greater part of the human race is content to live. The steadfast gaze of those melancholy eyes never wavered. It is not the cold blue Irish stare of a Bernard Shaw, unblessed by the slight astigmatism of common humanity. The difference may be seen by anyone who compares Augustus John's portraits of the two men where they hang in the Fitzwilliam Museum at Cambridge. The Irishman, with his strong neck and bristling brows and beard, seems to challenge the world's unreason to mortal combat, while the old man of Wessex watches it with the sad, still gaze of a lifelong unsurprise. It is the gaze of a man who had cared much but expected little; patient, undeceived, compassionate. In fact, the man who wrote on his eighty-sixth birthday

> Well, World, you have kept faith with me,
>   Kept faith with me;
> Upon the whole you have proved to be
>   Much as you said you were.[4]

The poet had never belonged to the Fabian Society, nor indeed to any club of the kind that exists to improve the world. He had cared for life as an emotion, not as a scientific game. If he had any politics, he once wrote, they were neither Tory nor Radical.

> Conservatism [he wrote] is not estimable in itself, nor is Change, or Radicalism. To conserve the existing good, to supplant the existing bad by good, is to act on a true political principle, which is neither Conservative nor Radical.[5]

He would, he said, prefer to call himself an 'Intrinsicalist'. He was equally opposed to democratic and to aristocratic privilege, and while he believed in equality of opportunity for all, he disliked the worse than aristocratic arrogance of those who think that hand-labour is the only labour, and he was against the taxing of those who help themselves in order to help those 'who will not help themselves when they might'. As for politicians a long experience of London society seemed to confirm the impression of Charles Dickens that they were chiefly concerned with the Boodle-Coodle-Doodle shuffle of offices, concerned, in fact with 'everything except the people for whose existence alone these politicians exist'. At Lord Carnarvon's dinner-table he listened with amaze to

> the intensely average conversation on politics held there by average men who two or three weeks later were members of the Cabinet. A row of shopkeepers in Oxford Street, taken just as they came, would conduct the affairs of the nation as ably as these.[6]

On the other hand he was acutely apprehensive of the arrogant vandalism of 'proletarian democracy'. In the nineties he had watched the crowds gaily traipsing round the priceless treasures of antiquity in the British Museum and reflected

> They pass with flippant comments the illuminated MSS. —
> the labour of years — and stand under Rameses the Great,
> joking. Democratic government may be justice to man, but
> it will probably merge in proletarian, and when these
> people are our masters it will lead to more of this
> contempt, and possibly be the utter ruin of art and
> literature.[7]

Hardy cared for life more than he cared for art; he could not
bear the company of people whose sense of 'art' led them to
lose all sense of art's subsidiary relation to existence.[8] But a
world where art and learning were despised as somehow
'unreal' offended against the values of a man who came from
a cultural tradition whose craftmanship was the offspring of
real living. He was, in fact, a reactionary in the best sense of
the word.

   Hardy's vision, then, was simple, direct, and passionate.
This is to say, it was poetic. It was the unobscured gaze of a
people who had few illusions and still fewer temptations to
indulge them. The visitor to Egdon may wake up to greet the
morning at eight and to rejoice that God is in his heaven and
all is right with the world. But the native has been up in the
dark with a lantern to milk the cows, and knows that God is
best praised in Stinsford Church on Sunday mornings.
Meanwhile, there is a full day's work to be done, and time
waits for no man. The earth and the sky change every
minute. The days pass away like water under a bridge, and
the night cometh when no man may work. Nature, to the
men and women who live close to it, is a flux, not a still-life.
The heart of man longs for pause, some fixed point of rest in
the everlasting course of things passing onwards. To stand
aside from the flux for a space, to pin down some moment
before it can chase away after all the rest, to escape from the
ceaseless rhythm of change and decay and renewal altogether: this would be paradise, if only it were not death. A
man might be pardoned, if he had time to think about it, for
wishing that he had not been born . . . But who harbours
such thoughts? The women, perhaps, who have time for such
things. Or a dreaming boy, freed by some chance to stand

and stare, aside from the flood of labour in nature's bosom. Such a boy was the young Thomas Hardy.

Among his earliest memories was one of lying on his back in the sun, with an old straw hat over his face, and deciding that he did not wish to grow up, or to possess things, but 'to remain as he was, in the same spot, and to know no more people than he already knew (about half a dozen).'[9] Defeatism, escapism, so says the glib modern commentator. It was neither. It was the temperament of the child of his place and his people: the longing of the child of hard-driven countryfolk to stay the sun in the sky, the leaf on the tree, the water in the stream. 'It is the on-going, i.e. the 'becoming' — of the world that produces its sadness', wrote the man who had grown out of the child, forty years on. 'If the world stood still at a felicitous moment there would be no sadness in it. The sun and the moon standing still on Ajalon was not a catastrophe for Israel, but a type of paradise.'[10] And again, a little later: 'To think of life as passing away is a sadness; to think of it as past is at least tolerable.' The dreamy, watchful child at Higher Bockhampton would cry when he saw the leaves falling in autumn. The man of fifty, looking at the landscapes in the Royal Academy, would note in his diary: 'All this green grass and fresh leafage perished yesterday; after withering and falling, it is gone like a dream.'[11] And when the eminent novelist made Father Time in *Jude the Obscure* explain his gloom at the flower-show by the reflection that all the flowers would soon be dead, he was transcribing into cold prose the common mood of the little boy who was father to the man, Thomas Hardy. The transcription is devoid of art. It grimaces at the reader from the page like a grotesque piece of the so-called 'Hardy-philosophy' — what has been called the philosophy of the disenchanted sophomore. But it is not that. It is a stubborn, unassimilated fragment of personal experience — the clumsy thumb-mark of a temperament.

'And still it moves . . .' Galileo's secret, jubilant reaffirmation of his heresy might have served as Hardy's lifelong lament. And what is it, after all, but the age-long lament of all poets and all poetry under the sun? 'Motion — change — mortality . . . Man cometh up like a flower . . . And thus we ripe and ripe,

and then we rot and rot . . . O death in life, the days that are
no more . . . Look thy last on all things lovely . . . And the
rotten rose is ripped from the wall . . .' But is there
anywhere, outside the life of this man, the record of a child
whose earliest conscious attitude towards the world was a
repudiation of change — a deliberate will not to grow up and
be a man? There are Peter Pans in plenty. Modern art is full
of them, mostly unconscious. And almost every creative
artist spends at least a part of his adult years in idealising the
eternal summer of his lost childhood. But Hardy reached the
stage of willing that his life, and that of the world, should
stand still, when he was little more than an infant. Nor was
his early life threatened with a sense of insecurity: he lived in
a peaceful, sheltered spot, his parents showered love upon
him, and his home was never burdened by want. Yet, in the
very morning of life, he looks before and after and longs for
the changeless in a world of change. At the opening of his
eyes upon the earth, when

> as a child I used to lie
> Upon the leaze and watch the sky . . .[12]

that mysterious voice from 'clouds and hills around' had
spoken of life's sad imperfection, and the voice became a part
of his being. It was from nature that it came — from 'clouds
and hills around' — from the world as a small mortal with a
poet's soul might see it from the edge of Egdon, where men
had loved and laboured and gone to their long rest for so
many centuries, where time's emblems looked out from every
ripening field, and man's mortality watched from every
barrow on the downs and every churchyard mound. The
youth was to read the *Essays and Reviews* of the Seven
against God, and Darwin and Huxley and Schopenhauer, and
he was to ask for the song of Old Omar Khayyam to be read
to him on his deathbed, far hence in the twentieth century.
But it began on Egdon. These sages were but part of the
pattern in the carpet which his personal idiosyncrasy bade
him watch. After all, they were of but secondary account in
his making. The temperament came first, and this sad theme
of time, and of life's inconsistency in the flux of things, was
its earliest as well as its deepest substance.

Thus the poet and the seer join the plain-spun man of country honesty and simple life, and the resulting complex is unique. A self-taught scholar-artist plodding his way to fame through sheer longevity we could the more readily understand, and some have thought of Thomas Hardy as little more than that. But the child of immediate vision, the youth of delicate perception, the mature man of finely sensitive inspiration — these characters succeed to the rest, and the product is of surpassing beauty. Slowly, like crystals forming upon a thread in a rich solution, the elements of this unique temperament coalesce into the pattern of the mature man and artist, and it is complete before he leaves his native heath for London and the world. Wessex is the solution, the immemorial culture of his home. The generations of his forebears lie heavy upon him, shaping the pattern of his soul with the strange pressure of hereditary compulsion. He knows where he belongs, the kind of people who made him, and he cherishes the theme of time's gift to himself, the latest of his line, like an inescapable destiny. Here, at least, is a constant: the recurrent features that he traced in his own physical being:

> I am the family face;
> Flesh perishes, I live on . . .[13]

But more than the face was the temperament, the residual qualities, virtues, loyalties, that came to him from his dear 'local hearts and heads'. And then — nature, and man's place therein. He had seen it from the beginning, and the child had wished to evade its threat of mutability. But the child became the man, and the man said what the child had seen and felt. The Wessex men around him scarcely knew of their lot. They lived their lives in toil and brief delights, for the most part accepting the burden of the flux of things without question and therefore without dismay. But if one had *seen* . . . ? If one had seen, perhaps, as the women saw, and here and there a dreaming boy? What then? To wish to stay the sun in heaven or the leaves on the tree were well enough for a woman or a child, but a man might make a song about it. To be a poet, to sing of chance and change, of time's revenges and the irony of kings and conquerors in their little hour of splendour? To tell the truth of the inner realities that lay behind the outward appearances and man's pitiful imaginings? To see the whole universe as Egdon might see it if only nature were conscious of itself? To be a poet like that, might it not be a way to subdue mutability itself?

The great artist, Coleridge once wrote, does what nature would do if the intervening obstacles were removed, which really means what nature would do if it were self-conscious, endued with a rational will. This is what Hardy did, and the nature which found in him eyes and ears and tongue, and most of all a heart, was a certain small patch of the English earth where his fathers had kept all these things inarticulate in their hearts from aforetime. 'All that Hardy felt and reasoned about mankind', writes Edmund Blunden, 'was founded in a particular appreciation of "local hearts and heads". His absolutes . . . were conjectured first and last from a profound submission to the diurnal, visible microcosm of Wessex. Even that term', Blunden wisely adds, 'in this regard may be too wide.'[14] It is too wide. It was from the family hearth, not to mention the family-tree, that Hardy's interest and affection proceeded outward to his native heath and from there to the kingdom of Wessex, the ancient nucleus of England, and from there to the nation, his country, and to the world. In every age of authentic culture the interests and affections of men have followed this natural order. It is what the Greeks meant when they claimed that their patriotism was founded upon the hearth. It is what Edmund Burke meant when he spoke of attachment to the subdivision, love of the little platoon, and the outward extending series of links by which we proceed towards a love to our country and to mankind. It is the truth celebrated by Coleridge in his apostrophe to the magic circle of neighbourhood:

In a circle defined by human affections, the first firm sod within which becomes sacred beneath the quickened step of the returning citizen . . . Here, from within this circle defined, as light by shade, or rather as light within light, by its intensity, and only within these magic circles, rise up the awful spirits whose words are oracles for mankind.

Thus is a temperament made, that mysterious constant like the family face,

> The eternal thing in man,
> That heeds no call to die.[15]

In one thing, at least, the man who grew from the child lying in the sunshine and longing never to change, was to triumph over time, for the work of such a man bears the sole passport to immortality.

4 The Gifts of Man - and Woman

A temperament is born, but the artist is made. A temperament, the peculiar psychical structure of an individual, is the product of a family and of a society, but there is no reason at all why it should issue in individual works of art. Before it can do this, it has to become self-conscious.

Primitive societies put their art into their crafts. In so far as they produce anything else, it flowers in the anonymity of ballad, folk-song and dance. No one 'made' the ballad of 'Sir Patrick Spens', or 'Greensleeves', 'The Western Tragedy' or 'The New-Rigged Ship'. These things represent the transmutation of communal experience by the creative imagination of whole peoples through many generations. Impersonal in style, devoid of moral reflections, nearly always melancholy in tone, their 'art' is like the fashioning of a curious stone by the sea. The particular and the inessential have been worn away, if indeed they ever existed, leaving only the essential, the universal, and the true. The effect upon them of time and anonymous human handling is equivalent to the effect of great poetic artistry, but the effect is not 'thought' by anybody in particular. They are the more or less perfect flower of the temperament, and of the way of life, of a society. It would be untrue to say that they are unconscious, but they are un-selfconscious. When such a society begins to produce individual artists, the spell is broken. The individual artist stands over against the society that bred him. He is conscious of himself as part of it, but he is also conscious of a certain detachment from it. He belongs to a world beyond: the world of intellectual knowledge, of conscious contrivance and individual reputation. Nor does he appear until the other world exists — until the society which bred him has a second world coming to life within itself. For there are not two worlds, but one. The world of Darwin and Huxley, of Pater and Henry James and

Meredith, was not planetarily different from the world of Wessex. The older world, which yet survived in Wessex, was their common parent. Egdon lies beneath Oxford, Box Hill, Belgrave Square, and even the South Kensington Museum. The new moon holds the old moon in its arms, but they are of one and the same body.

Art, like thought itself, is symptomatic of disease. Healthy beings, and healthy societies, do not think overmuch, nor do they produce individual artists. There are no mute inglorious Miltons. To be mute and inglorious is not of the nature of a Milton. Milton's was a highly conscious, not to say febrile, intellect, and the village community produces everything and anything but that. Only when the village community is in decline, when the ancient, largely unconscious society is breaking up and becoming something else, does it produce the conscious intellectually-seeking artist. The change overtakes different parts of a society at different times. Where the ancient constitution of society lingers longest, in something like health, there will the conscious individual artist be rarest; but when he does appear, either at the very turning-point of its fortunes or upon the outmost fringe of its contact with a more 'advanced' area, he is likely to bring with him a unique vitality, an original bearing, a freshness and profundity of vision that startles the old in sin, or the enlightened.

The bearer of this strange intruder from the past is always woman, and he will be found to live very much under the influence of Venus. For, in primitive societies, it is woman who takes the initiative towards thought and all that is normally meant by civilisation. D.H. Lawrence saw it happen on the edge of the industrial Midlands less than half a century ago, and recorded it forever in *The Rainbow*. First the men of the Marsh Farm:

> It was enough for the men, that the earth heaved and opened its furrow to them, that the wind blew to dry the wet wheat, and set the young ears of corn wheeling freshly round about; it was enough that they helped the cow in labour, or ferreted the rats from under the barn, or broke the back of a rabbit with a sharp knock of the hand. So much warmth and generating and pain and death did

they know in their blood, earth and sky and beast and green plants, so much exchange and interchange they had with these, that they lived full and surcharged, their senses full fed, their faces always turned to the heat of the blood, staring into the sun, dazed with looking towards the source of generation, unable to turn round.[1]

And then, the women:

The women were different . . . the women looked out from the heated, blind intercourse of farm-life, to the spoken world beyond . . . the women wanted another form of life than this, something that was not blood-intimacy. Her house faced out from the farm-buildings and fields, looked out to the road and the village with church and Hall and the world beyond. She stood to see the far-off world of cities and governments and the active scope of man, the magic land to her, where secrets were made known and desires fulfilled . . . she strained her eyes to see what man had done in fighting outwards to knowledge, she strained to hear how he uttered himself in his conquest, her deepest desire hung on the battle that she heard, far off, being waged on the edge of the unknown. She also wanted to know, and to be of the fighting host.[2]

Lawrence was transcribing his own experience into general terms, for he knew the same conflict within his father's house, the miner's cottage in The Breach, at Eastwood.

The colliers were deeply alive, instinctively. But they had no day-time ambition, and no day-time intellect. They avoided, really, the rational aspect of life. They preferred to take life instinctively and intuitively. They didn't even care very profoundly about wages. It was the women, naturally, who nagged on this score. There was a big discrepancy, when I was a boy, between the collier who saw, at the best, only a brief few hours of daylight — often no daylight at all during the winter weeks — and the collier's wife, who had all the day to herself when the man was down pit . . . The collier fled out of the house as soon as he could, away from the nagging materialism of the woman . . . He roved the countryside with his dog, prowling for a rabbit, for nests, for mushrooms, anything. He loved the countryside, just the indiscriminating feel of it. Or he loved just to sit on his heels and watch — anything or nothing. He was not intellectually interested . . . The woman almost invariably nagged about material things. She was taught to do it; she was encouraged to do it. It was a mother's business to see that her sons 'got on', and it was the man's business to provide the money.[3]

It is no wonder that Lawrence has written the only study of Thomas Hardy that gets below the surface. True, like everything else he wrote, it is mostly about Lawrence. Lacking Hardy's detachment, and therefore his compassion, Lawrence preaches his theme with the tedious castigatory hatred of a minor prophet. But he knew what he was talking about. It is the same theme: the death of an instinctive culture, and the tragic burden of increasing consciousness. Lawrence could never forgive the women for delivering the men over to the body of this death. From first to last he was the son of the Eastwood Congregational Chapel, and he spent the greater part of his life writing out the myth of the Fall, in the form of a theme with variations *con furioso*. And, of course, it all began with his mother, the 'superior' little woman who 'came from town, and belonged really to the lower bourgeoisie' and 'spoke King's English, without an accent, and never in her life could even imitate a sentence of the dialect which my father spoke . . . And she was very much respected, just as my father was not respected.' She was the woman who wanted 'another form of life than this', the miner's wife who, like the women of the Marsh, 'stood to see the far-off world of cities and governments and the active scope of man', and strained her eyes 'to see what man had done in fighting outwards to knowledge'. She was the representative of a generation.

My mother's generation was the first generation of working-class mothers to become really self-conscious . . . The woman freed herself at least mentally and ·spiritually from the husband's domination, and then she became that great institution, that character-forming power, the mother of my generation . . . in reaction against the ordinary

high-handed, obstinate husband who went off to the pub
to enjoy himself and to waste the bit of money that was so
precious to the family. The woman felt herself the higher
moral being; and justly, as far as economic morality goes.
She therefore assumed the major responsibility for the
family, and the husband let her. So she proceeded to
mould a generation.[4]

She got her way, and we got *Sons and Lovers.* Later, we
got *Aaron's Rod* and the revolt of Aaron Sisson against the
mother-wife complex, and, latest of all, the passionate
assertion of the male-principle and the restoration of the
woman to hearth and home. Lawrence claimed to have found
the organic society of balanced human relationships among
the Pueblo Indians. There, the woman has the property and
the children, while the man spends his real life in the Khiva,
the great sacred community of the men — a rather better
solution, Lawrence thought, than those twin bolt-holes, the
pub and the club.

> Let the woman take the children . . . Let the woman take
> the property — what has a man to do with inheriting or
> bequeathing a grandfather's clock! . . . And so, let men get
> free again, free from the tight littleness of family and
> family possessions.[5]

Hardy begins where Lawrence begins, but he ends not
among the Pueblo Indians but at the deathbed of Jude
Fawley. He was delivered from the dying culture of Wessex,
as Lawrence was delivered from the already dead culture of
the Marsh and the Erewash Valley, and for him, too, the
deliverance came at the hands of a woman. But the birth was
less painful. After all, it was still possible for a poet to live in
Wessex. The horrors of dissolution which drove Lawrence
from the Midlands, that festering 'scrabble of ugly pettiness
over the face of the land', the all-pervading smell of death
which turned him physically sick whenever he revisited it —
these things were as yet but a fetid taint on the wind blowing
from east of Andover. By 1850 Dorchester had a telegraph
and the London papers, and already in his boyhood Hardy
noted that the old country-songs were giving way to the

allegedly 'comic songs' imported from London. But Hardy could, and did, live in Wessex off and on for most of his life, and he was never to feel called upon to do more than protest a little sadly at the bad taste of 'church-restoration', or the pulling down of historic houses in the county town.

The domestic situation, however, was very similar to that of the Lawrences in the miner's cottage at Eastwood: the father and the mother drawn in opposite directions, the father to the instinctive life of the heath, the mother to the county town, the 'better' school for her son, the life of learning and conscious, rational power beyond the scope of Egdon. There was no drama in the situation, and hardly any open conflict, such as we find in *Sons and Lovers*. The boy was never torn by the antagonism of his parents, never took sides with his superior mother against his native father. The clash of the male and the female principles was never to inform his work as an artist with the doctrine. Jude was not to die of excessive cerebration, along with the cerebral new woman, Sue Bridehead, or because he failed to 'realise' himself with the splendid animal, Arabella Don. Even Clym Yeobright, who comes nearest to the Lawrentian victim of excessive cerebration, does not die of it, as Gerald Crich was to die among the snows.

Thomas Hardy senior, builder and life-renter in a remote village community, lacked the 'art of enriching himself by business'. He was a handsome, clear-eyed, gossiping person. His son was to liken him to Hamlet's Horatio, and one would suppose him to have been a rather more talkative version of Giles Winterbourne with perhaps a touch of Gabriel Oak about him. Had he been a little more alive to worldly opportunity he would have removed his business into Dorchester, but he never did. Lawrence speaks somewhere of how often he had seen a collier of his father's generation stand in his back garden looking down at a flower with the odd, remote sort of contemplation of the incipient artist, and he recalls how his father would come home from the night-shift at the pit in the early morning,

> happy because of his long walk through the dewy fields in the first daybreak . . . He watched every bird, every stir in

the trembling grass, answered the whinnying of the peewits
and tweeted to the wrens. If he could, he also would have
whinnied and tweeted and whistled in a native language
that was not human. He liked non-human things best.[6]

Such a man, translated into an unspoilt rural environment,
was the father of Thomas Hardy. He liked going off alone
into the heath and the woods with a telescope and peering
into the distance by the half-hour, or lying in the sun on a
bank of wild thyme among the grasshoppers. This side of his
father's life — the genuine, unintellectual attitude born of an
old, unhurried, passional way of life — the poet himself
inherited, along with the ambitious and enquiring spirit of his
mother. For all his careful apprenticeship to letters, his
craftsman's pains, his thirst for intellectual knowledge, he
tried always to experience life as an emotion, not a scientific
game. Writing his own elegy as he neared his eightieth year,
he wished chiefly to be remembered as 'a man who used to
notice such things' as the new-spun silk of the May month
leaves, the dewfall-hawk alighting upon the upland thorn, the
night-travelling hedgehog, and the bell-note broken by the
wind.[7]

Song and dance are the oldest, and the favourite, expression of the ancient culture of the land, and what
Thomas Hardy senior loved above all things was music-
making. Here again the Egdon native joins hands across the
shires with the black diamond of Eastwood. For, even in
Lawrence's twentieth-century boyhood in the English
midlands, the colliers still loved to sing and dance, and
Lawrence *père* was a great dancing-man in his youth. To this
day you may still hear the melancholy trumpet and the lively
piccolo playing from the parlours of the miners' cottages as
the menfolk practise for the weekend revels of the Colliery
Band. There sit the children of a disinherited peasantry,
shirtsleeves uprolled, foreheads bulging, sad eyes staring out
beyond the Nottingham-lace curtains of the woman's 'little
home', as they make music over the grave of a departed
civilisation. The Hardys, back in mid-century Dorset, knew
no such drear confinement even though, as we know from
Under the Greenwood Tree, the curtain was falling on their

musical activities in the parish church. They jigged and
fiddled and danced and sang, in the kitchen and the parlour,
at the lane-end and in the village street, and, for as long as
they were able, they carried their fiddles and viols and
serpents to church on Sundays. Little Thomas had his fiddle
as soon as his hands were big enough to hold a bow — his
father saw to that — and he fiddled away at jigs and reels,
waltzes and hornpipes, with the best of them. Soon he was
going the round from farm to farm, playing at bridals and
harvest-suppers, at mumming plays and Christmas wassailings.
He remembered always the bride stooping in the candlelight
to kiss the little fiddler of the reels, and the night when he
played 'The New-Rigged Ship' so fast and for so long that the
hostess laid hold of his bow-arm in fear that he would burst a
blood-vessel. And then the long trudge home across the snow
at three in the morning, and the drunken man whom he
helped his father to drag from a snowdrift. The mother seems
to have had little patience with her menfolk's passion for
music making. It diverted her husband from his duty of
getting on in the world, and she tried to put a brake on her
son's eager progress in the track of his father's muse. But it
was no good, and she knew it. Still, Mrs Hardy insisted that
her son should on no account receive payment for his services
at feasts and bridals. Once, at least, this injunction was
secretly disregarded, and Tom bought *The Boys' Own Book*
with the proceeds.

It is typical of Hardy that this book was still in the library
at Max Gate at his death. Perhaps it stood for him as a
memento of something that went very deep into his life and
character: the gift of his father.

> The dance it is a great thing,
>   A great thing to me,
> With candles lit and partners fit
>   For night-long revelry;
> And going home when day-dawning
>   Peeps pale upon the lea:
> O dancing is a great thing,
>   A great thing to me![8]

The dance was a passion with him. He danced in the early

days at Higher Bockhampton and Weymouth, and he danced in the more sophisticated circles of London, as we learn from his poem, 'Reminiscences of a Dancing Man'. Even the most trivial Victorian measure held a lure for him. The elusive tune of a certain quadrille which he had heard at Dorchester in his youth haunted him like a passion. Emma Hardy used to tell a story of seeing her husband in the summer of 1878 running down the street 'without a hat'. He had heard a street barrel-organ playing that very quadrille, but the grinder was a young foreigner who could not identify it. These airs had a power to stir him to the depths of his being. When, in his middle fifties, the eminent novelist led off the first figure at the Pitt-Rivers' house-party with the beautiful Mrs Grove, did he perhaps remember how the child, dancing to his father's fiddle in the kitchen at Higher Bockhampton, would stop suddenly at a certain modulation with tears in his eyes? He had not known why certain music always made him sad, though the fact had set him wondering about himself. Later, he was to come upon the secret in his beloved Shelley: 'Heard melodies are sweet, but those unheard are sweeter . . .' and the inmost echo of the mystery in the voice of Wordsworth: 'The still, sad music of humanity . . .' That is what he had been hearing all the time, a deep life beyond the life of the mind. Perhaps it was what his father heard when he lay out in the sunshine on Egdon and listened to the grasshoppers, or the distant collier when he sat on his heels and watched — anything or nothing. Life, after all, consisted for the men not in facts but in a flow, and life for Thomas Hardy should be an emotion and not a scientific game. If there were a pattern in the flow, a rhythm in the emotion, it was far more likely to be the pattern and the rhythm of a quadrille, where all the dancers ended up in the place where they had started, than a procession headed by the Prince Consort and Mr Darwin along the road of inevitable progress. 'History,' wrote Hardy, at forty-five, 'is rather a stream than a tree'.[9]

Thus far the gifts of the father. But young Hardy was his mother's son, too. His father had given him a toy concertina and then a fiddle. His mother gave him Mr Cassell's *The Popular Educator*. She also gave him Dryden's *Virgil*,

Johnson's *Rasselas,* and *Paul and Virginia,* and she saw to it that he got some French from the lady who taught his sister. While the father's steady humorous gaze looks at us from his portrait and seems slightly to mock at the world beyond Egdon with all the serenity of an older wisdom, the mother's face looks at us from her portrait with the authentic gaze of the woman who strains her eyes 'to see what man has done in fighting outwards to knowledge . . .' She came of the numerous family of the early-widowed Elizabeth Swetman, herself a woman of unusual ability and judgement, who had married a poor man for love. Elizabeth Swetman toiled hard for her children and sought solace in books. She was, through her books, an intellectual influence in the early life of her grandson. 'We are such stuff as our grandmother's dreams are made on.'[10] It is unlikely that Elizabeth Swetman had much time for dreams, for many years, but she set the intellectual tone for the Hardy family. We are told that she knew the writings of Addison and Steele and other of the *Spectator* group almost by heart, and she was thoroughly familiar with Richardson and Fielding, *Paradise Lost* and *The Pilgrim's Progress.* These books were in every house where literacy prevailed in eighteenth-century England (Elizabeth Swetman was born in 1778), and it prevailed in far more houses than the latter-day champions of education are sometimes willing to admit. Gabriel Oak had among his books *Paradise Lost, The Pilgrim's Progress,* and *Robinson Crusoe.* A fragile and precocious child, given like Hardy to brooding upon mutability from earliest days, could find ample food for its musings in an environment so supplied, and always it came to him at the hands of the women. It was the grandmother who set the tone, the mother who set the direction and the aim.

There is no evidence that Jemima Hardy thought poorly of her husband's trade, or that she wished to push her clever precocious son on to a higher social level. The fortune of a master-builder who employs his own labour and lives securely, if not affluently, in a pleasant house within three miles of a county town, is not to be despised. Nor was there any question of the Hardys 'emancipating themselves from the feudal system'. Although the local Lady of the Manor

was still a great power in the life of the village community,
Thomas Hardy senior was not dependent upon her favour for
his livelihood. The Hardys were neither peasant nor servile.
They belonged to that great section of the rural population —
ranging from village craftsmen, small traders and tranters,
down to turf-cutters, drovers, reddlemen and squatters —
whose existence blurs the neat lines of 'the manorial system'
and is scarcely recognised by textbooks on economic history,
or by Marxist literary critics. Like so many others of their
kind, great and small, the Hardys lived on the manor but not
exclusively by it. Thus, when Jemina Hardy offended Her
Ladyship by removing her son from the local school to a
school in Dorchester, the master-builder found that less
business on the estate came his way in future, but he was not
ruined, nor even much impoverished. He could, and did, look
elsewhere, though with less energy than would have pleased
his wife. But it must have been plain to Jemima, in one way
or another, that there was no future for her son in the family
business, aside altogether from the boy's promise as a scholar.
So she got him to school in the county town, and thereafter
into the drawing-office of Mr Hicks, the architect. No doubt
it was a 'step up' from building to designing, from master-
builder to architect, but there was never any question of the
mother fighting for her son to 'have his chance', as
Lawrence's mother fought for the young Bert to get out of
the miner's cottage at Eastwood to the Nottingham High
School. Thomas Hardy was not exactly born with a pen
behind his ear, but he came of a social order where you had
only to walk behind a goose long enough to be sure of
picking up a quill.

   A great deal of nonsense has been written about Hardy's
education. He had all the instincts of the scholar, and he
loved scholarship for itself. He could equally well have
become a don or a divine. The fact that he did not has
nothing to do with lack of opportunity. The notion that he
was a Jude Fawley — that *Jude the Obscure* was the
embittered autobiography of a frustrated scholar — is readily
disposed of by the most summary reading of *The Life of
Thomas Hardy*. His own note in his journal tells us of the
germ of *Jude:*

A short story of a young man — 'who could not go to
Oxford' — His struggles and ultimate failure. Suicide.
There is something [in this] the world ought to be shown,
and I am the one to show it to them — though I was not
altogether hindered going, at least to Cambridge, and could
have gone up easily at five-and-twenty.[11]

Putting aside for the moment the all-important question of
his cultural environment, Hardy had the typical formal
education of the average middle-class English boy from
Tudor to late Victorian times. That is to say, he went to the
village school and then to an 'Academy' — an institution
synonymous with (and at Dorchester in the 1850s, superior
to) a Grammar School. It was an education at least equal to that
of Shakespeare or Sir Walter Scott, and a good deal better than
that of Dickens or H.G. Wells. It included friendship at an
early age with men as distinguished as William Barnes, Horace
Moule and Arthur Blomfield, and he was fortunate in his
teachers. He had an excellent Latin master and was well
grounded in the language of both Virgil and Homer. Nor did
he ever relinquish his classics. 'Read some more Horace' is the
diurnal entry in the diary of the young Hardy in London.
Homer, Virgil, Aristophanes and Theocritus all figure in his
year's reading-record at the age of forty-seven. The influence
of the classics on *The Return of the Native* has been pointed
out by more than one critic. The novelist who ended *Tess* in
Aeschylean phrase was not indulging in a piece of classical
exhibitionism but making ready (perhaps too ready) reference to the reading habits of a lifetime. Hardy read the Greek
and Latin authors all his life because he loved them, because
they had something of everlasting veracity to say to him. For
the rest, his schooling gave him proficiency in drawing and
mathematics: he became an able draughtsman, and he got to
know as much arithmetic, algebra and geometry as is good
for a man. The old academies and grammar schools still
neglected modern languages, but Jemima Hardy didn't. It was
his mother who sent him to lessons with a French governess
and bought him Cassell's *The Popular Educator* so that he
could begin the study of German. Though we are told that he
was, mercifully, a rather idle schoolboy, he nevertheless

approached manhood more than amply equipped to cope with whatever problems he was likely to meet in the pursuit of a professional career in Victorian England. He was, moreover, endowed with a keen sense of history by his classical and architectural studies.

5 Portrait of the Artist as a Young Man

Thomas Hardy was not a peasant, nor did he come of a peasant family. It is doubtful whether there were ever any peasants in England. Sometimes one gains the impression that the country has been exclusively populated from the earliest times by an infinitely sub-divided middle class. Hardy was a countryman who lived the typical life of a working novelist of the Victorian Age. He is no more, and no less, usefully described in class terms than Charles Dickens.

The first thing that strikes the reader of *The Life of Thomas Hardy* is the breadth and variety of Hardy's experience. The notion put across by Virginia Woolf in her obituary essay in 1928 that his life was 'lived simply down in Dorsetshire' is about as accurate as Hazlitt's famous portrait of Jeremy Bentham as 'The hermit of Queen Square Place'. The error in both cases arises, at least in part, from the same largely physical circumstance: that of longevity. Bentham lived to eighty-five; Hardy lived to eighty-seven. Both men outlived almost all their distinguished contemporaries. Choosing to live their later years in the physical seclusion appropriate to elderly gentlemen, they were readily endowed with eremitic propensities by the younger generation who knew very little of their earlier lives. In fact, neither Bentham nor Hardy ever ceased to take a keen interest in the affairs of a rapidly changing world. Whom the gods love die young in another sense than in years. Bentham, according to John Stuart Mill, was a boy to the end. Hardy married again at seventy-three, and at eighty-seven wrote a lyric to a girl he had seen at fifteen. The purely temporal parallel between the two men's lives might be carried further without irrelevance. They were both born within twenty-five years of the close of a great European war, and in the middle years of their respective centuries. They both passed their early lives in a period of social equilibrium and lived to see the world of their youth disrupted by war and revolution. They both outlived the tumult and the shouting of the latter-day apocalypse and died on the eve of events that must have seemed in their childhoods as remote as Babylon or Troy: Bentham in the year of the Great Reform Bill; Hardy within five years of the installation of Adolf Hitler as German Chancellor. To Bentham, the doctrinaire philosopher, historical perspective was as nothing; to Hardy, the poet of *Time's Laughingstocks and Revenges,* it was almost everything.

A man's life has a certain shape. It could with a little ingenuity be drawn roughly on a graph. Hardy's would look like this:

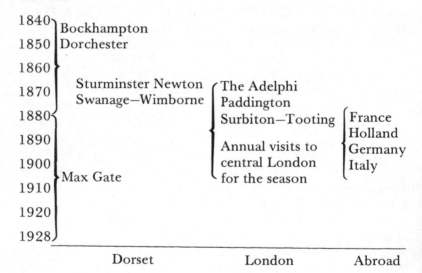

1840	Bockhampton		
1850	Dorchester		
1860			
1870	Sturminster Newton	The Adelphi	
	Swanage—Wimborne	Paddington	
1880		Surbiton—Tooting	France
1890			Holland
		Annual visits to	Germany
1900		central London	Italy
1910	Max Gate	for the season	
1920			
1928			
	Dorset	London	Abroad

Plainly this is not the life-graph of an Egdon 'native'. Even the 'Egdon Period' — the first twenty-two years — was spent partly in the county town of Dorchester. From twenty-two to thirty-four, a twelve-year span at the most vigorous period of most men's lives, Hardy was very largely a Londoner. At his marriage (which was celebrated not under the greenwood tree, but at St Peter's, Paddington), he took his bride not to Dorset but to Surbiton, after a honeymoon on the Continent. After Surbiton, they stored their worldly goods in four small wooden boxes and took furnished lodgings at Westbourne

Grove in West London. Thence they wandered in Bohemian fashion, taking lodgings at Swanage and Yeovil, until family opinion was heard to hint that they 'appeared to be wandering about like two tramps'. One day in 1876 they went out and bought a door-scraper and a bookcase at an auction sale and decamped to a pretty cottage at Sturminster Newton. There they actually stayed for two years. Then came another spell in, or near, London: three years at Upper Tooting. In June 1881 they moved to Wimborne, and in 1885 to the newly-built Max Gate. This, if any, date marks the return of the native. The local lad who left Egdon at twenty-two to seek his fortune in London has made good. At the age of forty-five he builds himself a house on the edge of his native town, a kind of New Place beside the west-country Stratford, and there he lives for the rest of his days, with annual visits to London for the 'season' and occasional trips to the continent of Europe, where his interest in history was fed by visits to battlefields and monuments of the past. Not until he neared his eightieth year is there any question of Thomas Hardy 'living quietly in Dorsetshire', and even then the Virginia Woolfs and Siegfried Sassoons and T.E. Lawrences were to be continually knocking at the door of Max Gate.

Certain facts stand out in this life-history of the mortal clay of Thomas Hardy. First and foremost is the fact that he spent the most formative years in the best possible place for a poet to spend them — in the country, and yet within easy reach of a county town. In this, his earliest youth, his heart and mind lay open to the beauty, the peace and the natural rhythm of country things. This is the aspect of his life that everyone knows about: Hardy far from the madding crowd. The second aspect is less well known: Hardy the young man with his living to make in Victorian London. For several years he worked at an office, first in St Martin's Place and then in Adelphi Terrace, hard by London's 'central roar'. He spent his lunch-hours at the National Gallery; he supped at Covent Garden; he danced at Almack's; he went to Drury Lane for drama and to Exeter Hall for oratorio; he attended classes in French at King's College and improved his mind in the Reading Room of the Kensington Museum; he sampled

Divine Service at a dozen London churches on Sundays; and
he played Italian opera on an old fiddle, and wrote poetry, in
his lodgings in Westbourne Park Villas. All through these
years he was, in all externals, the average young office man of
Victorian London whom Charles Dickens was even then
immortalising in the renowned Swiveller and the egregious
Guppy. He wore a beard, a curly-brimmed bowler hat, an
overcoat like a sack, and he never missed a chance to improve
his mind or to rejoice in a quadrille. The young Hardy must
have known his London as only a country-bred sojourner gets
to know it. There is nothing like living in lodgings in
Westbourne Park Villas for seeing the macrocosm in
microcosm and for getting rid of any illusions one may
possess about the universal significance of cows and peasants.
As D.H. Lawrence pointed out, Egdon Heath lies under
London, Paris, and even New York; but you only see that
when you have lived in Westbourne Park Villas.

Thirdly, there is the Bohemian element about Hardy's
course. The young man from Dorset emerges from the
London years as a novelist, and takes to himself for wife the
sister-in-law of an Anglican parson. They marry in a London
church, and they live for a time at Surbiton, and they seem
all set for the 'villa chastely grey' of the 'worthy pair, who
helped advance sound parish views' in Hardy's poem 'The
Conformers'. But there is a period in which they change
house or lodgings about six times in as many years. It is clear
that between Surbiton (1874) and Upper Tooting (1878) the
Hardys were a restless pair, forever packing up their
possessions to go somewhere else. Physically, this period of
Hardy's life ended when they left 'Riverside Villa', Sturminster Newton, for Upper Tooting on 20 March 1878. 'End of
the Sturminster Newton idyll', Hardy wrote in his diary at
that time; and later he was to add, 'Our happiest time'.[1] It
was in 1879, early in the Upper Tooting sojourn, that he felt
that 'there had past away a glory from the earth', and we
read in the *Life* that ' . . . it was in this house that their
troubles began'. He was thirty-nine. He had been married for
five years. The *wanderjähre* were over, and the eminent
novelist was coming reluctantly to his moorings. Even at
'Riverside Villa' he had complained to his diary of 'The

irritating necessity of conforming to rules which in themselves have no virtue'. A few days later, he looked out of the
window in the middle of the night to see their servant coming
out of the out-house with a man who was about to be let into
the house through the back door, which was found later to
have been oiled. Emma ordered the girl to bed; but next day
she ran away, and a little later they heard that she was to
have a baby. 'Yet never a sign of one is there for us', wrote
the author of *Life's Little Ironies,* who was sleeping in Holy
Wedlock with Emma Lavinia.[2]

Which brings us to the last outstanding fact about Hardy's
pilgrimaging: its almost complete lack of drama. It is true
that an effort has been made of late to supply him with a mis-
tress when he was a young man and when he was seeing a good
deal of a young woman called Tryphena Sparks, and, to
complete the story, to equip him with an illegitimate son.
Perhaps it was hardly to be hoped that a 'permissive' society
could allow the 'good little Thomas Hardy' to be all that
good. Besides, there was his famous 'pessimism' which had to
be accounted for by some secret sorrow. Tryphena Sparks,
who was Hardy's cousin and lived at Puddletown, has been
tracked down as 'The Unknown Beloved', and the still more
unknown bastard has been christened Randy, all on
account of an ancient dame who was Tryphena's daughter by
the man she married after parting with Hardy. And to make
things more enthralling, it is said that Tryphena was not − as
we once supposed − Hardy's cousin but his niece. It might
have been imagined − it *was* indeed imagined − that incest
would come into the story somewhere. The aged Mrs Nellie
Bromell, who died at eighty-six, expatiated on the story we
are told, for the benefit of the authors of that strange book
Providence and Mr. Hardy. Strange not because of anything
inherently impossible about its story − there are poems
which make it clear that Hardy did have an emotional
involvement with Tryphena − but because its authors see the
'lost prize' − Tryphena − appearing again and again in his
writing. To imagine that such 'revelations' throw light on the
causes of the notorious 'pessimism' of the poet, or that he
spent his life covering up his tracks while transmitting a
lifelong series of cryptogrammatic messages to the lost

beloved, reveals a quite remarkable obtuseness about what
T.S. Eliot meant when he said, with a poet's authority on the
creative temperament and the creative process: 'The more
perfect the artist, the more completely separate in him will
be the man who suffers and the mind which creates.'[3] The
obsessive need to go poking into private affairs upon which
time has cast its merciful blankness confuses rumour and
surmise with fact, and would certainly have offended Hardy's
historical sense and his shrewd grasp of the difference
between fact and fiction.

Hardy's parents lived into extreme old age. Apart from the
early death of Horace Moule, he never experienced the loss of
a beloved friend. Indeed, he would appear to have been a
man of many acquaintances and few friendships. His married
life declined from its first 'mad romance' into an affair of
mutual tolerance and grumbling irritation; there was estrange-
ment, as we know from the 'Poems of 1912-13', but there
was no breach. The twain converged in rapture and then
somehow contrived to go their own ways in double-harness.
Dividing every year between Dorset and London, they dined
out and paid calls, attended 'crushes' and public gatherings.
In the country there were Shakespeare-readings with 'the
wealthy Mrs. B impassive and grand in her unintelligence,
like a Carthaginian statue', and 'The General' reading his part
gingerly for fear of blurting out one of the Bard's indecen-
cies.[4] At Max Gate, Thomas wrote his novels upstairs while
Emma Lavinia fiddled about in the garden at 'the end of the
alley of bending boughs'. When novel-writing days were over,
Thomas composed *The Dynasts* while Emma composed
poems about pet cats for the poets' corner of the *Dorset
County Chronicle*. So the years passed. So, perhaps, the lives
of most authors pass. It is only in the twentieth century that
the ignorant have come to believe that to be a poet one must
be a drunkard and a lecher. The really strange thing about
Hardy's life is that this particular author was living all the
time in the stormy hearts of Tess Durbeyfield and Jude
Fawley, or soaring on the wings of the Ironic Spirit far above
the fleets and squadrons of the Napoleonic Age.

The life-course of Thomas Hardy, then, follows a fairly
familiar pattern: a childhood and youth spent in a remote

and beautiful countryside; a young manhood as the industrious apprentice in the capital city of his native land; a
period of earnest striving, continual self-improvement and
clerkly respectability; a romantic love-affair in the thirties,
accompanied by a certain Bohemian restlessness of the young
artist and his wife; the arrival of success in his chosen trade of
letters, accompanied by the process of settling down to a life
divided between town and country; and finally the declining
years of the Doyen of English Letters at a quiet house on his
native heath. It is not unlike the life of William Shakespeare,
with the Anne Hathaway affair coming after instead of
before the fortune-seeking in London. It was certainly no
more and no less dramatic than the life of Shakespeare (so far
as we know anything about the latter) in the elements of
personal action, and probably rather richer in opportunities
for personal observation of the human scene. It was no more
the life of an Egdon native than Shakespeare's was the life of
a native of Stratford, and no less.

But the point is that both men were natives of *somewhere*
Warwickshire or Wessex, and while they lived lives of broad
and varied experiences, they both brought to that experience
the instinctive values of the society which bred them.
Moreover, it was the same society. A common culture linked
sixteenth-century Warwickshire and early nineteenth-century
Dorset in a bond which has scarcely a thread of communica-
tion with the rootless urban agglomerations of the twentieth
century. It was out of this common culture of old English
society that Shakespeare could speak to the whole audience
of the Elizabethan theatre in the language of their common
life. Hardy spoke from the selfsame culture in an age when
that society had been blasted at the root and driven back to
the secluded depths of ancient Wessex. Even there it was fast
disappearing before the invading armies of progress, the
Farfraes, the Fitzpiers's, the Alec d'Urbervilles. The Great
Western Railway reached Dorchester in 1847, and Hardy
himself assisted Professor Smith is designing schools for the
London School Board set up by Mr Forster's Act· of 1870.

Hardy was unfortunate in the circumstances of his elegiac
utterance. Raising his voice in the heyday of Victorian
prosperity, he was easily and readily labelled a pessimist. For,

however considerably the Victorian compromise had been
shaken by the scientists, a leader in life and letters was still
unaccountably expected to celebrate some kind of 'far-off
Divine Event, to which the whole Creation moves'. Victorian
England could take the death of King Lear because that was
'Shakespeare'. It could take 'Thoughts that do often lie too
deep for tears' because Wordsworth, after all, wrote the
Ecclesiastical Sonnets. But when it found itself judged by a
man from Wessex who called it 'spectral', a society of ghosts,
heartless in its human relationships and largely automatic in
its cherished activity, it quickly made up its mind that the
man, while he might be a good story-teller, was merely
jaundiced in his 'message'. The reviewers did not really assert
'This is an untrue and inartistic view of life', but 'This is not
the view of life that we people who thrive on conventions can
permit to be painted'. He had seen it all so clearly when he
wrote 'In Tenebris' in 1895-6.

> Let him in whose ears the low-voiced Best is killed by the
> clash of the First,
> Who holds that if way to the Better there be, it exacts a
> full look at the Worst,
> Who feels that delight is a delicate growth cramped by
> crookedness, custom, and fear,
> Get him up and be gone as one shaped awry; he disturbs
> the order here.[5]

Intent on establishing himself as a novelist and as 'a good
hand at a serial', he felt compelled to manhandle his plots in
order to make a living by story-telling in the Victorian world
of progress. When in the end he felt secure enough to give
them the whole truth as he saw it, they turned and rent him.
Yet the tragedy of Tess and of Jude is neither more nor less
'pessimistic' than that of Hamlet or Lear. The vision sprang
from the same country-bred, London-fostered intelligence
looking with clear eyes upon the tragedy of the human spirit
at disastrous odds with the brute facts of the flesh,
circumstance and an indifferent universe. The gods who
finished their sport with Tess were permitted to send polite
shivers down the spines of ladies and gentlemen in the stalls
at Drury Lane so long as they were likened to 'wanton boys',

and Jude was permitted to curse the day he was born so long as he did it in church. It was time that someone spoke out from Egdon. This was the 'silenced' novelist who had learned to live in 'unhope', who wrote *The Dynasts: le dernier cri* of Thomas Hardy.

His youth had laster a great deal longer than most men's. It is wrong to think of him as always the 'time-worn' man of Augustus John's famous portrait of him at eighty-three. This shows a head carved as if from an ancient stone or modelled from an ancestral bird. Its appropriate inscription would be the verses with which he concluded his first volume of poems in 1898:

> I look into my glass,
> And view my wasting skin,
> And say, 'Would God it came to pass
> My heart had shrunk as thin!'
>
> For then, I, undistrest
> By hearts grown cold to me,
> Could lonely wait my endless rest
> With equanimity.
>
> But Time, to make me grieve,
> Part steals, lets part abide;
> And shakes this fragile frame at eve
> With throbbings of noontide.[6]

In 1892, when he was fifty-two, he looked into his glass after hurting a tooth, and was struck by 'the humiliating sorriness of my earthly tabernacle'. It was sad, he said, that 'the best of parents could do no better for me . . . ' It was just one more example of nature's failure to keep up with the human spirit. All his life he was aware of this. He was, he said, a child until he was sixteen, a youth until he was twenty-five, a young man until he was nearly fifty. A clue to much of his character and action throughout his life, he thought, was afforded by his lateness in virility while mentally precocious.

He was always in love. First, with the lady of the Manor when he was nine or ten; then with a girl on horseback who chanced to smile at him as he came out of school, and whom he sought for, and got his friends to seek for, over a whole week before he got over 'this desperate attachment'. There was Louisa in the lane, though he never spoke to her — save to murmer once, 'Good evening', and there was Lizbie 'Browne' of the beautiful bay-red hair to whom he wrote a poem after she had lived in that 'encysting' memory for more than thirty years. On 1 March 1888 we find him writing down his recollections of 'four village beauties', of whom Lizbie is one. These and many more lie behind the note he made when a young man in London: 'Walked about by moonlight in the evening. Wondered what woman if any, I should be thinking about in five years' time.'[7] Then there was the ubiquitous Tryphena, and Florence Henniker, and when he married Florence Dugdale at the age of seventy-three he made provision in his will for 'the first child of mine who shall attain the age of twenty-one'. Hardy's marriages were, however, childless, though we owe to Lois Deacon the immortal line, 'he was probably not altogether without issue'. The second Mrs Hardy became seriously alarmed by her aged husband's infatuation with Gertrude Bugler who had delighted him by her playing of Tess in the dramatised version of the novel at Dorchester in 1924. Love is the overriding subject of his poetry, and the finest of these love poems were written when he was more than seventy. Time did indeed shake the fragile frame at eve with throbbings of noon-tide, for it is true that they whom the gods love die young. Hardy died young at eighty-seven. As the landlord of the 'Phoenix' tavern said with a happy smile when asked if he could remember his fellow-townsman: 'Mr Hardy was fond of the ladies.'

His gallery of fair women in prose and verse is immortal and immensely varied, and there is at times an outspokenness in his poems dealing with the relationship between men and women — as, for example, in that remarkable 'One Ralph Blossom Soliloquizes' — which shows that he was, indeed, able 'to express more fully in verse ideas and emotions which run counter to the inert crystallized opinion . . . which the vast body of men have vested interests in supporting.'[8] Edmund Gosse once said of Hardy, 'He is a wonder if you like. At eighty-seven and a half without a deficiency of sight, hearing, mind or conversation. Very tiny and fragile, but full of spirit and gaiety not quite consistent in the most pessimistic of poets.'[9]

'Really the thing is prodigious', Rebecca West exclaimed about the famous pessimism. 'One of Hardy's ancestors must have married a weeping willow.'[10] The wife of his old age knew better. Florence Hardy was once described by Siegfried Sassoon as a person who enjoyed being gloomy, but it was she who wrote to a friend in the last year of the poet's life, 'He is now — this afternoon — writing a poem with great spirit: always a sign of well-being with him. Needless to say it is an intensely dismal poem.'[11] She would have recognised her husband more readily in Somerset Maugham's Edward Driffield accompanying himself on the banjo in the music-hall song describing the beating-up of 'The Man who Struck O'Hara'[12] than in Miss Deacon's suffering lover of the lost Tryphena Sparks. In his eightieth year he seized a fiddle and played for the dancers at a party. 'He did not dance', Florence Hardy recalls, 'but he was longing to, I could see, and would have footed it as bravely as any.' With Hardy we have always to reckon with the public *persona* which comes between the man who suffers and the artist who creates. Florence herself was enough of a creative artist to understand this, as Miss Deacon is not. So was Sir Henry Newbolt. 'Dear old T.H.', he said. 'He's tried all his life to be a pessimist, and some fine ancestral Tom (au*tom*aton = the unconscious self) has kept the fire alight in the basement all the time.'[13] It is to the 'fine ancestral Tom' that Rebecca West is referring when after her reference to the ancestral weeping willow, she says that 'the customary condition of Thomas Hardy's mind was an abundant appreciation of life'. She can feel, in reading such a scene as that of Sergeant Troy's sword-drill,

> The most complicate system of joys circling within joys, like the stars dancing among themselves in the heavens: a joy in the earth itself, in bodies, in beauty, in strength, in sex . . . joy in the peacock strut of the male, joy in that aspect of the woman which must be symbolised by a moist, pouting, dark rose lower lip . . . [14]

It is the lip which he insists on, again and again, in Tess, and he writes of, 'The irresistible, universal, automatic tendency to find sweet pleasure somewhere, which pervades all life . . . '[15] This was what Hardy's unconscious pleasurably saw in life, this and the other joys he sings of in 'Great Things', but because it was so habitual it did not leap so easily to the recalling memory. He does not write about the warmth which his sound blood, the blood which kept him going for most of a hundred years, sends through his veins. Rather he writes about the time when the blood seemed shocked out of his body by the chill air that rose from an open grave. Hence those many records of mere calamity, of charnel accident, which are merely the distortions of a great quality, shadows which must be cast by a strong light, nothing to be counted against him.

It is here that we come nearest to the answer to one of the most perplexing questions of Hardy criticism; why are so many of the tales and poems of this son of the smiling, fatalistic race of Wessex folk concerned to tell us 'how an unenjoyable time was had by all'? Wessex folk themselves are sometimes sorely perplexed, indeed repelled by it, for the customary response to Hardy in Dorchester is well portrayed in a remark overheard in the streets during the Thomas Hardy Fesitval in 1968. Hardy was 'the miserable old fellow who went about with his eyes on the ground and had never a good word for us . . .' The fact is that Hardy told the kind of stories that country people tell each other — again we remember the old ballads — and when country folk do that it is always what Rebecca West calls the 'fractures' of one's normal life that appear first. They remember first what was not customary. And Hardy, the professional writer, did the same, and took it for granted that it was the thing to do. Time after time the point is to be found in the notes he made for the more profitable exercise of his trade:

> The real, if unavowed, purpose of fiction is to give pleasure by gratifying the love of the uncommon in human experience.[16] . . . a story *must* be striking enough to be worth telling. Therein lies the problem — to reconcile the average with that uncommonness which alone makes it natural that a tale or experience would dwell in the memory and induce repetition.[17]

That was the trouble with the 'slice of life' writers. They forgot 'that a story must be *worth the telling,* that a good deal of life is not worth any such thing . . . ' As George Gissing, who was deeply influenced by Hardy, was one of the first to point out, Hardy was no 'realist', and Gissing was an authority on that subject.

Hardy in his grasp of the relationship of fact and fiction, history and myth, showed himself to be far more perceptive and intelligent than some writers of the mid-twentieth century who have published articles and books of so-called history based far too largely on Victorian works of fiction. *Hard Times* is a great novel but it should not be regarded as a completely reliable source-book for factual studies of Victorian education, as it so often is. There is a sense in which a great novel is a great source of truth, but this truth is almost always overlooked by those whose approach is glib and facile and who know little of the true disciplines of history. That Hardy wrote so much about suffering and unhappiness should not be regarded as indisputable evidence that at the time at which he was writing everyone was unhappy most of the time. This school of 'fictional historians' should remember the opening words of Hardy's speech when he was presented with the Freedom of Dorchester:

> . . . I may be allowed to confess that the freedom of the Borough of Dorchester did seem to me at first something that I had possessed a long while . . . for when I consider the liberties I have taken with its ancient walls, streets, and precincts through the medium of the printing-press, I feel that I have treated its external features with the hand of freedom indeed . . . Nevertheless, when somebody said to me that 'Casterbridge' is a sort of essence of the town as it used to be . . . I could not absolutely contradict him, though I could not quite perceive it. At any rate, it is not a photograph in words, that inartistic species of literary produce, particularly in respect of personages.[18]

6   *The Trumpet-Major*

The Trumpet-Major has been called 'a prelude to the mighty business of *The Dynasts*'. It was this only in the limited sense that its story was placed in the year of the invasion threat of 1805, and, in the author's words, 'founded more largely on testimony — oral and written — than any other in this series'. The external incidents which direct its course, Hardy goes on to say, 'are mostly an unexaggerated reproduction of the recollections of old persons well known to the author in childhood, but now long dead, who were eye-witnesses of those scenes'.[1] The novel represents, therefore, a peculiarly Hardyan type of history, history derived from 'living documents'. He admits at once, however, to the difficulty experienced by anyone who attempts to construct a coherent narrative of past times from the fragmentary information furnished by survivors. For 'the articulation of a skeleton' he had recourse to newspapers and even books. *The Trumpet-Major* was written more than twenty years before the great Epic-Drama, when Hardy was thirty-nine, less than half-way through his career as a novelist. Of his major works, only *Far from the Madding Crowd* and *The Return of the Native* were before the world, and he was very much concerned to win readers by writing stories for a large audience in his quest for bread and butter. It was still possible for a reviewer to imagine himself to be paying him a considerable compliment by predicting that Mr Hardy seemed 'to be in the way to do for rural life what Dickens did for that of the town'.[2] The novel was on the whole favourably received. It had come out serially in *Good Words* and Mrs Grundy had secured the transference of a love-scene from a Sunday to a Saturday and the omission of one or two oaths. Leslie Stephen had declined *The Trumpet-Major* for *The Cornhill Magazine* (which had carried *Far from the Madding Crowd* and *The*

Hand of Ethelberta as serials) when Hardy told him that it was to be a historical novel which introduced George III. 'I think that a historical character in a novel is almost always a nuisance',[3] he said.

George III in *The Trumpet-Major* is an unmitigated success, as he was to prove in *The Dynasts*. 'Thank God, I have seen my King!', says Mrs Garland when the royalties have passed by. 'What a good brave King!', says Anne Garland when John Loveday tells her that the King is anxious to fight Boney single-handed. 'Long live King Jarge!', cries the crowd. Even if all they see, like Anne, is a profile reminding them of the current coin of the realm, this is the cheerful red-faced old gentleman who lives with his loyal subjects by the summer sea, and rejoices to see them enjoying themselves at singlestick and grinning through horse-collars. Hardy leaves us with the unforgettable picture of the King talking kindly to Anne about her sweetheart after she has watched the *Victory* sail past Portland on the way to Trafalgar. Next to the King in historical importance is Captain Hardy, Nelson's flag-captain, stepping out of a brown curricle as he goes to see the King at Gloucester Lodge on the Esplanade, 'a hale man, in the prime of life, wearing a blue uniform, gilt epaulettes, cocked hat and sword . . .' From his drawing-room at Max Gate Hardy looked out at Captain Thomas Masterman Hardy's monument at Blackdown Hill above Portesham. He belonged to the novelist's lineage. T. E. Lawrence used to urge Thomas Hardy to have his own monument set up somewhere in sight in case people got confused between the two, which has happened, even though Kennington's bronze effigy of the little man in cycling-breeches sits at the top of Dorchester town ironically looking down at a never-ending succession of twentieth-century traffic snarl-ups. These figures, the 'good old King' and Nelson's flag-captain, were familiars of his youthful background, local hearts and heads, if only by adoption. The inn which was opened beside Max Gate at the Hardy Festival of 1968 bears the sign 'The Trumpet-Major'.

The notebook in which Hardy collected his materials for *The Trumpet-Major* ('and other books of time of George III' says his inscription on the front cover) is lodged in the

County Museum at Dorchester. It has been carefully collated with the novel, and with *The Dynasts,* by Dr Emma Clifford.[4] The bulk of Hardy's notes were made at the British Museum from newspapers and magazines, especially *The Morning Chronicle, The Morning Post* and *The Gentleman's Magazine.* Other material is copied from Regimental Standing Orders and from the Proclamations of the period, to which Hardy had access at the Dorset County Museum. Notable among this material is the 'Address to all Ranks and Descriptions of Englishmen' which he reproduces entire in Chapter 23, calling upon all men to engage themselves as Volunteers for the defence of the nation against 'your old and implacable Enemy', a stirring call for a levy *en masse* familiar enough to anyone who can remember the inception of the Local Defence Volunteers, known later as the Home Guard, in the great crisis of a later age. Hardy also made use of a number of contemporary volumes, especially *The Adventures and Recollections of Colonel Landmann* (1852), from which he took details of military and naval dress. His greatest standby, however, was the work to which he acknowledges his debt in the 1895 Preface, C. H. Gifford's *History of the Wars of the French Revolution* (1817). From this he lifted almost bodily the humorous description of the local volunteers' drill-parade in Chapter 23. When he was later charged with plagiarism he was to do little more than refer to Shakespeare's use of North's Plutarch and avow that Gifford's account closely accorded with 'the local traditions of such scenes that I have heard recounted, times without number'. After all, his grandfather had drilled with the volunteers at Weymouth! Carl J. Weber looked into this matter of Hardy's plagiarism and his research illustrated Hardy's superior respect for oral testimony and local tradition.[5]

As for the places, for much of his life he had only to look outside his front door. In 1879, however, he was living at Upper Tooting, and he had to journey down to Dorchester and Weymouth in order to warm his mind at the originals of Overcombe Mill (Sutton Poyntz) and Oxwell Hall (Poxwell Manor). The latter, the home of old Squire Derriman, or Uncle Benjy, was to be described in one of Hardy's most successful set-pieces in Chapter 6:

The rambling and neglected dwelling had all the romantic excellencies and practical drawbacks which such mildewed places share in common with caves, mountains, wildernesses, glens, and other homes of poesy that people of taste wish .to live and die in. Mustard and cress could have been raised on the inner plaster of the dewy walls at any height not exceeding three feet from the floor; and mushrooms of the most refined and thin-stemmed kinds grew up through the chinks of the larder paving. As for the outside, Nature, in the ample time that had been given her, had so mingled her filings and effacements with the marks of human wear and tear upon the house, that it was often hard to say in which of the two or if in both, any particular obliteration had its origin. The keenness was gone from the mouldings of the doorways, but whether worn out by the rubbing past of innumerable people's shoulders, and the moving of their heavy furniture, or by Time in a grander and more abstract form, did not appear. The iron stanchions inside the window-panes were eaten away to the size of wires at the bottom where they entered the stone, the condensed breathings of generations having settled there in pools and rusted them. The panes themselves had either lost their shine altogether or become iridescent as a peacock's tail. In the middle of the porch was a vertical sun-dial, whose gnomon swayed loosely about when the wind blew, and cast its shadow hither and thither, as much as to say, 'Here's your fine model dial; here's any time for any man; I am an old dial; and shiftiness is the best policy.'

Here is history at work, or 'never-napping Time' at its tiny chisellings, as Hardy was to describe it in later years.[6] *The Trumpet-Major* is full of such recordings, among which is notable the description of Overcombe Mill itself in the second chapter.

As for Budmouth, Hardy had lived in lodgings at Weymouth as a young architect ten years before. There he had rowed in the Bay and gone dancing and written many of the scenes of *Desperate Remedies*. The evocation of the Georgian watering-place in Chapter 13 of *The Trumpet-Major* was the bringing to life of sites and scenes which to him must still have been very near the surface more than seventy years after the departure of King George and the military. He had still by him the manuscript of his first unpublished novel, *The Poor Man and the Lady,* and he did not hesitate to plagiarise himself as well as C. H. Gifford. Probably very little of *The Trumpet-Major* is taken from *The Poor Man,* but the opening of Chapter 23 is taken almost word for word from the opening of Chapter 12 of *Desperate Remedies.* After all, *The Trumpet-Major* must have been very easy to write, and it is certainly very easy to read. Carl Weber was unwise to say that Hardy 'lacked sympathy with the spirit of historical romance', and that 'this novel has never stirred readers deeply and it never will.'[7] It is redolent of Hardy's own young days by the sea and has a freshness and charm unmatched by anything outside the pages of *Under the Greenwood Tree,* which is saying a great deal. Perhaps Michael Millgate has put his finger on the real source of the novel's appeal for some readers when he writes, 'Overcombe can thus be seen as a pastoral microcosm juxtaposed to, and eventually engulfed by, a macrocosmic world of great events', and he goes on to show how the events of the novel are made 'all the more poignant for the haunting awareness of violence and danger close at hand'.[8] The great historical backcloth is seldom absent for long in a Hardy novel.

History is faithfully portrayed in *The Trumpet-Major* within the small scope of a few square miles of Wessex in the days when George III was King and Napoleon Bonaparte was regarded by the King's subjects as the 'junior gentleman of the two arch-enemies of mankind'. In fact, it is Hardy's solitary piece of historical reconstruction in the proper use of that term. It is improper to mention it in the same breath as *The Dynasts,* which is not only an infinitely greater work in every sense but an enterprise of a quite different order, only historical in its accoutrements, not at all in its intention. Hardy does not use the word in his title. In his Preface to *The Dynasts* he simply calls the work, a 'Spectacle . . . presented to the mind's eye in the likeness of a Drama . . . concerned with the Great Historical Calamity or Clash of Peoples, artificially brought about some hundred years ago.'

That the spectacle or the drama should have been concerned with that particular historical calamity was decided by the accident of propinquity. It happened to be the one that he, Thomas Hardy, knew most about. It might have been another. The principal characters are not Napoleon or George III, Nelson or Pitt, but certain Phantom Intelligences, 'supernatural spectators of the terrestrial action', for whose entertainment the drama is performed, and whose comment upon it ensures that it shall possess a certain dreamlike quality. It is only a slight overstatement to say that *The Dynasts* was performed as part of the education of the Spirit of the Pities. Hardy saw his work not as belonging to firm-footed Clio, but as a play of 'poesy and dream', with monotonic delivery of speeches, with dreamy conventional gestures, something – as he himself said – 'in the manner traditionally maintained by the old Christmas mummers'.[9]

The Trumpet-Major is nothing like this. Its action is slow – Arnold Bennett described it as 'excessively slow' – its scenes loaded with detail, much of it taken straight from the carefully assembled items of the *Notebook*: from Queen Charlotte's appearance as 'a little old woman, small black silk bonnet, and the remainder of her person covered by a short plain scarlet cloth cloak' (which is Hardy's note from Colonel Landmann's *Adventures and Recollections*) and her six cream-coloured horses (as in the note he took from *The Morning Post*) down to the personal appearance of Captain Hardy and to the King going out of his way to salute the sentries in his blue coat and gilt buttons. It would be untrue to say that so lightsome a story ever plods, but it often has something of the prosy weight and deliberation of narrative history. Not that anyone is appointed to point the pictures like a lantern-lecturer with his cue, as the Spirits frequently do in *The Dynasts*. Hardy is careful to make us feel that the vicissitudes of Anne Garland and her suitors are much more important than the fate of the country while we are reading about them. Only once does he explicitly make the reader reflect that his chief characters exist in a great historic, even worldwide drama, when Anne Garland herself reflects upon it for a moment:

Anne now felt herself close to and looking into the stream

of recorded history, within whose banks the littlest things
are great, and outside which she and the general bulk of
the human race were content to live on as an unreckoned,
unheeded superfluity.[10]

In a historical novel, or in history, people don't do this kind
of thing. The reader is immersed in history from beginning to
end and the history is no backcloth. If the reader gets out
onto the bank and gazes at the stream he begins to gasp like a
fish, the illusion is destroyed, and we feel that we would be a
great deal better off with poetry and with cosmic presences
pointing out things to us and uttering the appropriate
reflections. When Hardy does this in the passage already
referred to in Chapter 5 of his novel, suddenly speaking *in
propria persona,* telling us that: 'There is not one among
them [the guests] who would attach any meaning to
"Vittoria", or gather from the syllables "Waterloo" the
remotest idea of his own glory or death', and adding that the
correct and innocent Anne scarcely thought 'what things
Time has in store for her at no great distance off' — then we
feel that we, and he, in the particular context of this novel,
are floundering on the bank. Here is the typical contrast with
the Hardy of *The Dynasts* who is on the bank all the time.
When the Spirit of the Pities ventures to associate himself for
a moment with the sufferings of the wretched puppets he is
promptly called to order by the Spirit of the Years:

> The ruling was that we should witness things
> And not dispute them. To the drama, then.[11]

Because Hardy was the poet who, twenty years later, was to
write *The Dynasts,* it was hardly to be expected that he
would write an historical novel like Sir Walter Scott. It is true
that one of his first actions when he set out to write *The
Trumpet-Major* was to buy a set of the Waverley Novels in
forty-eight volumes, but it is significant that he preferred
Scott the poet to Scott the novelist. To him, Sir Walter was
the poet who wrote *Marmion,* and he came to regret that the
author of 'the most Homeric poem in the English language —
Marmion — should later have declined on prose fiction.'[12]
Signs of the epic-poet in *The Trumpet-Major* are to be found

only in the passing reference to Anne's momentary awareness of 'the stream of recorded history' when she watches the soldiers saluting the King on the Esplanade at Weymouth, and in the heavy-handed reference to the innocence of future battles on the part of the soldiers at the Miller's party. There is also the elegiac passage, replete with *sic transit gloria mundi,* as the spectators come away from the Review on the downs:

> At twelve o'clock the review was over, and the King and his family left the hill. The troops then cleared off the field, the spectators followed, and by one o'clock the downs were again bare.
>
> They still spread their grassy surface to the sun as on that beautiful morning not, historically speaking, so very long ago; but the King and his fifteen thousand armed men, the horses, the bands of music, the princesses, the cream-coloured teams — the gorgeous centre-piece, in short, to which the downs were but the mere mount or margin - how entirely have they all passed and gone! — lying scattered about the world as military and other dust, some at Talavera, Albuera, Salamanca, Vittoria, Toulouse, and Waterloo; some in home churchyards; and a few small handfuls in royal vaults.[13]

The military and other dust which is to be scattered about the world is history; but the worms of Waterloo, the butterflies and snails, the coneys and moles, awaiting the 'foul red flood' on the night before the battle, as

> The eyelids of eve fall together at last,
> And the forms so foreign to field and tree
> Lie down as though native, and slumber fast![14]

— these are poetry. The provenance of the novel is England, and England's heart, Wessex. The provenance of the epic-drama is Europe, the world, the cosmos.

7 The End of Fiction

Novel-writing as an art cannot go backward. Having reached the analytical stage it must transcend it by going still further in the same direction.

Thomas Hardy, 1886.[1]

Hardy was to go on writing novels for another fifteen years or so after *The Trumpet-Major.* When, after *Jude the Obscure,* he gave up novel-writing, he had had a good run for his money. He had been at it for nearly thirty years. By the time he was forty-five he had made enough money to buy land and build himself a house at Max Gate, close by the county town. He had just written *The Mayor of Casterbridge,* an appropriate celebration of his intention to live there. He had resigned himself to novel-writing as a regular trade, though he had never wanted to carry it on as such, being committed to it by circumstances, as he had previously been committed to architecture. He went about the business efficiently, living in London for a part of each year, going into society, keeping a record of his experiences in social life, and using his wit and genius to produce great novels in spite of the oppressive Victorian pressures on writers who wished to handle adult subjects. To some extent he was relieved when the uproar over *Jude the Obscene* encouraged him to drop novel-writing, although it was 'a smart and amusing' review of *Tess* in the *Quarterly* at the expense, he complained, of veracity and sincerity, which elicited his often-quoted remark that 'if this sort of thing continues, no more novel-writing for me. A man must be a fool to deliberately stand up to be shot at.'[2] Such 'misrepresentations', as he called them, simply compelled him out of self-respect to abandon a form of literary art which he had long intended to abandon at some indefinite time and 'resume openly that form of it which had always been more instinctive to him'. Even in his novels he had, as he tells us, kept his subjects as near to poetry 'as the conditions would allow'. As early as 1875 he had been impressed by a letter from Coventry Patmore regretting that the beauty and power of *A Pair of Blue Eyes* 'should not have assured themselves the immortality which would have been impressed upon them by the form of verse'.[3] But at that time he was committed to prose - his attempts to get his poetry published in the 1860s had met with no success — and Patmore's message sent him, like the studious craftsman he was, to a fresh reading of the great English prosodists in order to cultivate a prose-style.

The fact that his success as a novelist, a success which was ironically made all the greater by the 'scandal' associated with *Tess* and *Jude,* meant that he could at last afford to turn to poetry, must not be allowed to conceal the fact that he was moved by other and less commercial considerations. He was coming to think that it might be possible to express more fully in verse ideas and emotions which ran counter to 'the inert crystallized opinion — hard as a rock — which the vast body of men have vested interests in supporting.'[4] To utter such ideas and opinions in poetry might cause people merely to shake their heads, especially in England where poetry was never taken seriously by the generality, whereas to argue them out in prose was like drawing up an affidavit, and at once made them sneer — or at the worst dismiss the writer as a 'harmless agnostic', or as 'a clamorous atheist, which in their crass illiteracy they seem to think is the same thing . . . ' Hardy ventured to suggest that 'If Galileo had said in verse that the world moved, the Inquisition might have let him alone.'[5] Even more, he had been for some time coming to the conclusion that the novel was played out, that it was 'losing artistic form with a beginning, middle, and end, and becoming a spasmodic inventory of items, which has nothing to do with art.'[6] We have already seen how, in 1886, looking at the Bonington painting on the wall of his drawing-room, he had decided that he didn't want to see scenic paintings of landscapes and that the 'late-Turner rendering is now necessary to create my interest'. The parallel between his views on art and what he was finding out about the realistic novel is striking, but to be expected. The analytical novel could only go on being more and more analytical, *ad infinitum,* and he personally had no interest in such a course. In order to be true to his vision he would have to write another kind of novel altogether, if he were to write novels at all. *Tess* and *Jude* were the end of the old road for him. In his last published novel of all, *The Well-Beloved* — an underrated work because it is called a novel — he wrote a book that fits nowhere in his course as a novelist and yet is deeply interesting because it is an attempt to do in prose what would have been best done in poetry. In the Preface he wrote for it in 1912 he described it as a story which differed from all or most others of the series 'in that the interest aimed at is of an ideal or subjective nature, and frankly imaginative, verisimilitude in the sequence of events has been subordinated to the said aim.' In another place he explained that *The Well-Beloved* had been sketched many years earlier when as a young man he had been interested in the Platonic Idea, which, 'considering its charm and its poetry, one could well wish to be interested in always'.[7] The word 'poetry' is the keyword here. The idea was the subject of a poem called 'The Well-Beloved' in *Poems of the Past and the Present* (1901) and perhaps it is a pity that Hardy ever tried to treat it in prose. Not only has *The Well-Beloved* been regarded askance in most studies of Hardy's novels, it was soundly abused on its publication as a novel and at least once — as Hardy put it — with 'mendacious malice'. Writing to Swinburne, Hardy said:

> I should have added that *The Well-Beloved* is a fanciful exhibition of the artistic nature, and has, I think, some little foundation in fact. I have been much surprised, and even grieved, by a ferocious review attributing an immoral quality to the tale. The writer's meaning is beyond me.[8]

It was as much this experience as any which ended his prose contributions to literature and killed all his interest in this form of imaginative work, which had ever been secondary to his interest in verse.

Ultimately, he realised that it was the best thing that could have happened. In the middle of December 1898 *Wessex Poems* was published. Two years later came *Poems of the Past and the Present,* and over the next thirty years another six volumes of his poetry were published (comprising well over 900 poems in all) together with the Epic-Drama of *The Dynasts,* consisting of three parts, nineteen acts, and one hundred and thirty scenes, and *The Famous Tragedy of the Queen of Cornwall,* a verse-drama in twenty-four scenes. Many of the poems in his recollections had been composed back in his youth and early middle age and 'From an old copy' is a common note at the end of them, while sometimes he gives two dates, 'begun — ', and, 'finished — ', the two dates lying twenty, thirty or even forty years apart. The stream of poetry now poured forth, and it is to be doubted whether any poet of high quality ever put forth so much in so short a time. Hardy, however, had the prolificity that goes with genius in general. He was, too, a confirmed 'book-maker', and hated to throw away anything that would help to swell out another volume. It is untrue to say that we ought to regret this, for the least of his poems bears his unique character, like the faint five hundredth carbon-copy under the hand of a master. We can learn as much about Hardy from his worst as we can from his best work, and sometimes more. Some of the most unkind criticism of his poetry at the time of its publication, particularly of the first two books of verse which were, of course, published before *The Dynasts,* amounts to little but umbrage on the part of the critics that he should have taken the liberty of adopting another vehicle of expression than prose-fiction without consulting them. It has been said, not untruly, that a writer can do anything he likes as long as he goes on doing the same thing. As early as *The Hand of Ethelberta,* which followed immediately on his first real success with *Far from the Madding Crowd,* Hardy had been made (as he puts it) 'aware of the pecuniary value of a reputation for a speciality'. Now he needed to bother no longer.

When the time came to write *The Dynasts,* in the first years of the new century, Hardy was tackling a subject that had been in his mind for a quarter of a century. His first notebook entry on the project was in 1875 when he envisaged a series of ballads on the war with Napoleon, 'forming altogether an Iliad of Europe from 1789 to 1815'.[9] By 1877 the idea has advanced a stage further 'from that of a ballad, or ballad-sequence, to a 'grand drama', viz . . . a grand drama based on the wars with Napoleon . . . '[10] It were better to say, not that Hardy chose the subject, but that the subject chose him. In his Preface of September 1903 he immediately declares that the subject has been determined by three 'accidents of locality'; the writer's familiarity with a certain part of England, the proximity of this district to the invasion coast, and the neighbourhood of the village where Nelson's flag-captain at Trafalgar had been born. It was a region animated by memories and traditions of the year 1805 which, for Hardy, seemed still to hang in the air. Straightway, when he sat down to write, even before visiting the seats of government in Paris and London, and immediately after encountering the aerial presences of the Overworld in the Fore Scene, he descends upon 'A Ridge in Wessex', the beloved soil whence, Antaeus-like, all his strength was drawn.

'I should not think of devoting less than twenty years to an epic poem', Coleridge once said. 'Ten to collect materials and warm my mind with universal science . . . ' including mechanics, hydrostatics, optics, astronomy, botany, metallurgy, fossilism, chemistry, geology, anatomy, medicine, the mind of man and the minds of men, in all travels, voyages and histories. 'So', he went on, 'I would spend ten years — the next five to the composition of the poem — and the last five to the correction of it'. Needless to say, he never wrote an epic poem. Hardy spent his twenty years of preparation in writing novels. Ezra Pound saw the poems as the harvest of having written the novels first. Hardy warmed his mind on Egdon Heath, and, as Edmund Blunden has pointed out, 'his absolutes . . . were conjectured first and last from a profound submission to the diurnal visible microcosm of Wessex.' There in the microcosm he found the macrocosm. And as in writing a novel it was ever his assiduous habit to visit the scenes of his story, so in writing *The Dynasts* he visited 'history' by reading a great many history books. Some of the books he read, as he said afterwards, were 'very long and not very good,' so that he was wont to add 'you may be sure I have not read them since'.[11] However, they had enabled him to collect a lot of material, and 'it seemed a pity not to make use of it'. Like a good craftsman he was anxious not to waste anything, and he prided himself on the historical accuracy of *The Dynasts,* for what it was worth. In a work of great length and complexity he has never been seriously faulted, and anyone intent on textual research can track down the historical record of each and every scene almost line by line.

In his Preface, Hardy acknowledged his indebtedness to the 'abundant pages of the historian, the biographer, and journalist, English and foreign'. This gracious acknowledgement refers explicitly to 'all cases outside oral tradition, accessible scenery, and existing relics'. The really important materials, which (to use Coleridge's words) warmed his mind, lay precisely within those three categories. He could and he did wade through the twenty volumes of Sir Archibald Alison and Monsieur Thiers, of Capefigue and Lanfrey and Ségur and Napier, but the things that set his mind alight were 'An outhouse door riddled with bullet-holes . . . a heap of bricks and clods on a beacon-hill . . . worm-eaten shafts and iron heads of pikes . . . ridges on the downs . . . '[12] He once noted down his opinion that 'An object or mark raised or made by man on a scene is worth ten times any such formed by unconscious Nature.'[13] Clouds, mists, mountains, all were unimportant compared with 'the wear of a threshold, or the print of a hand'. *Humani nihil a me alienum puto.*[14] What Coleridge called 'things contingent and transitory' stirred Hardy more deeply than any example of the written or printed word. He could never have crossed the plain of Marathon, as Coleridge said he could, 'without taking any more interest in it than in any other plain of similar features'.

He was a born battlefield hunter, moved to his depths by the spirit of place. Not only did he visit the obvious haunts of the sightseer like the field of Waterloo. He spent hours of a continental holiday trying to locate the site of the Duchess of Richmond's ball at Brussels, which, as he reports in a footnote to *The Dynasts,* proved as elusive as towered Camelot or the hill of Calvary. It was the same, or worse, when he tried to ferret out the Bridge of Lodi, since the young Scotch officer of Foot who accompanied him cheerfully avowed that he had never heard of it. Apparently to some people the historical associations of a place were a positive obstacle to higher thoughts. Shakespeare's mulberry-tree, the room in Carnarvon Castle where the Black Prince was born, the rock by the seashore where Giordano Bruno hid from his pursuers — to take pleasure in these things, Coleridge said, except for amusement or the gratification of curiosity was like the superstitious reverence of pilgrims staring at a great man's shin-bone surviving unmouldered in his coffin. It degraded the sacred feeling. For the human mind had the privilege of abstracting pure ideas — 'things of now, for ever, and which were always' — from all that is material and transitory. So much the worse for Coleridge, who was almost entirely lacking in historical sense and a sufficient grasp upon substantial reality. In all this he proudly proclaimed his dissimilarity from Sir Walter Scott, for whom every old ruin, hill, river or tree called up a host of associations. The two things, historical sense and attachment to substantial reality, go together.

Hardy's attachment to the substantial world in all its detail was like that of the race from which he sprang: life-renters, village craftsmen, 'makers' in every rural material from seasoned timber and quarried stone to calf-skin and neats' leather. He happened to make books and he brought to book-making the handicraft, the 'touch' of his race. Thomas Carlyle's father was a master stonemason, too, and when Carlyle was a famous man he one day took hammer and chisel to renew the lettering on his father's grave-stone. Thomas Hardy was always prepared to recommend a tombstone-maker or an obituary-memorialist to his friends, some of whom, then and later, have shown a strange surprise at his concern with, almost his devotion to, the furniture of churches and graveyards. He not only designed his own house at Dorchester but the memorials to his choiring ancestors in the church at Stinsford, and to his first wife at St Juliot, not to mention the memorial to

THE
FAMOUS DOG
WESSEX
August 1913–27 Dec. 1926
Faithful. Unflinching.

in the garden at Max Gate. Thus it was in his poetry, too. He
never neglected the local association, the reference to the
Hardys who had 'haunted nigh.' He could not refrain even in
a ballad like 'A Trampwoman's Tragedy' from bringing in the
family association with the celebrated horse-thief, 'Blue
Jimmy', stealer of more than a hundred horses before he was
caught, 'among others one belonging to a neighbour of the
writer's grandfather'. Blue Jimmy had come thus near to
Hardy, just as Hardy had come near to Marie Antoinette.
Many of his poems justified themselves in his mind on no
other ground than their enshrining of some item of local
gossip. He was capable of defending many a trivial and
unusual story with the innocent protest, 'But it *happened*
. . . ' adding perhaps that his father, or some neighbour, had
told him about it. And the *Life* and notebooks are studded
with 'strange' stories that Hardy has heard or read of. As that
other Thomas, also a village stonemason's son, once wrote in
his essay on 'Biography', 'Let anyone bethink him how
impressive the smallest historical *fact* may become, as
contrasted with the grandest *fictitious event* . . . The Thing
which I here hold in my mind did actually occur!'

Historic fact could have no better credentials than this:
that a thing happened, and that its happening was vouched
for by eye-witnesses. Such was the basis of all historical
writing in the earliest phase of the Western world. 'The work
of Herodotus or Thucydides', writes R. G. Collingwood,
'depends in the main on the testimony of eye-witnesses with
whom the historian had personal contact.'[15] After all, they
had little else to go on, and Collingwood would attribute 'the
extraordinary solidity and consistency of the narratives
which Herodotus and Thucydides finally wrote about fifth-
century Greece' to their method of using the testimony of
eye-witnesses. The limitations of the method, as well as its
advantages, are obvious. They were tied by a tether whose
length was the length of living memory. A modern man using
such a method, assuming him to be writing at the very end of
the nineteenth century, would be restricted to the period
since the French Revolution. This is precisely Hardy's
position. Born in 1840, he was growing up when survivors of
the Revolutionary and Napoleonic Age were rising seventy,

like his father's mother with her memories of the execution of the Queen of France. He had listened as a boy to the talk of men who had kept watch beside the Ridgeway beacon with its fine view over Weymouth, and in London in 1878 he had shaken hands and talked with a pensioner of eighty-eight at Chelsea Hospital who had marched in the Peninsula campaign. 'It was extraordinary to talk and shake hands with a man who had shared in that terrible winter march to Coruña, and had seen Moore face to face.'[16] On a yet earlier occasion he had been in the private parlour of 'The Turk's Head' at Chelsea with the pensioners 'where . . . over glasses of grog, the battle was fought yet again by the dwindling number of pensioners who had taken part in it . . . '[17] In his father's cottage at Bockhampton he had found in an old closet *A History of the Wars,* a periodical which his grandfather had subscribed to at the time, having been himself a volunteer:

> The torn pages of these contemporary numbers with their melodramatic prints of serried ranks, crossed bayonets, huge knapsacks, and dead bodies, were the first to set him on the train of ideas that led to *The Trumpet-Major* and *The Dynasts.*[18]

History was not merely something in a book. It was alive and was all about him at Higher Bockhampton. 'Here probably began Thomas's extensive acquaintance with soldiers of the old uniforms and long service', we read in the *Life* after a description of Hardy as a young boy attending a harvest-supper to which non-commissioned officers from the Dorchester barracks had been invited as partners for the girls.[19]

Hardy's distance in time from the scenes of *The Dynasts* was ideal for his poetic purposes. Tolstoy wrote *War and Peace* almost exactly fifty years after the Retreat from Moscow, and he was then between thirty and forty. It was fifty years after the events described in *The Dynasts* that Hardy's deep interest in them evolved, although it was to be another forty years or so before he made use of them in his epic-drama. It is sometimes said that the most difficult period of history to write about is the period a generation before one's birth. Difficult in the sense of its inaccessability to the imagination, it would seem. Such a period, it is supposed, lacks the total strangeness of more distant ages, and thereby lacks total challenge, while it still possesses sufficient proximity, or common ground, to perplex and baffle with treacherous comparisons. In fact, however, the situation is immensely favourable to the imaginative writer because of the survival of 'living documents', actors surviving from bygone scenes who bear with them the scent and echo of a drama which has hardly yet fallen to total silence. Hardy was in living contact with the history of more than a hundred years, and all his work — not merely the great Epic Drama or the one avowedly historical novel — is properly 'historical'.

On the other hand, being primarily a poet, and possessing an inherently philosophical turn of mind, he was entirely devoid of the superstitions of the 'professional' historian. More especially was he sceptical about the worth of historical documents. Beyond the articulation of a skeleton they were worthless as compared with oral tradition. 'Is not the present quasi-scientific system of writing history mere charlatanism?'[20] he asked himself while writing the best of his own truly historical novels, *The Mayor of Casterbridge,* in 1884, twenty years before J. B. Bury's famous declaration in his Inaugural Lecture as Regius Professor at Cambridge: 'History is herself simply a science, no less and no more.' The charlatanism was to be discovered in the historian's pretence of tracing events and tendencies, in the words of Hardy,

> as if they were rivers of voluntary activity, and courses reasoned out from the circumstances in which natures, religions, or what-not, have found themselves. But are they not in the main the outcome of *passivity* — acted upon by unconscious propensity?[21]

History, he would say, is a stream rather than a tree. 'There is nothing organic in its shape, nothing systematic in its development.'[22] He sees it flowing on like a thunder-rill by a roadside with a straw turning it this way and a tiny barrier of sand that, and with some commonplace mind in high office taking an offhand decision which may influence the course of events for a hundred years.

The best fiction, he was inclined to think, having written a good deal of it, 'is more true, so to put it, than history or nature can be'. The distinction between the historian and the poet (a term which embraces the greatest novelists who, like Hardy, are poets) is not that one writes prose and the other verse but rather, as we have seen before, that the historian deals in particulars while the poet deals in universals. It was for this reason that in his Apology to *Late Lyrics and Earlier,* in 1922, Hardy described poetry and religion as touching each other. As Aristotle put it, poetry is something more philosophic, and of graver import, than history.

8　The Historians

We have seen that Hardy's first note on the project which was to become *The Dynasts* referred to it as an Iliad of Europe. That was in 1875 when he was thinking of a ballad sequence. Professor J. O. Bailey has pointed out that as part of this plan he wrote the five poems, 'Valenciennes', 'San Sebastian', 'Leipzig', 'The Peasant's Confession' and 'The Alarm', which appeared in *Wessex Poems* in 1898. By the summer of 1877 there had been a great advance on his first plan and he was writing of a 'grand drama' based on the wars with Napoleon, which might be called 'Napoleon'. He had recently been consorting with the old soldiers at Chelsea Hospital. He had met Old Waterloo veterans at the sixtieth anniversary of the battle, and stored up in his memory the account of the old campaigner, John Bentley, and of how he and his comrades had slept, wet and hungry, on the eve of the engagement: a reminiscence which was to occupy a footnote to Scene viii of Act VII, thus putting John Bentley of the Fusilier Guards on record as the typically Hardyan 'authority'. At this time he also visited the scene of the battle. In 1880, lying in bed for several months with internal bleeding, he had abundant time to think about his project, and the most important development is recorded in the note:

> Mode for a historical Drama. Action mostly automatic; reflex movement, etc. Not the result of what is called *motive*, though always ostensibly so, even to the actors' own consciousness. Apply an enlargement of these theories to, say, 'The Hundred Days'![1]

On 16 February 1882 a further note appears:

> Write a history of human automatism, or impulsion — viz., an account of human action in spite of human knowledge,

showing how very far conduct lags behind the knowledge that should really guide it.[2]

This was to be a theme which occupied his mind increasingly from this time forth. The incipient drama of *The Dynasts* became a philosophical poem, something beyond the reach of the analytic novel whose limits, he thought, had now been reached. The Creatures of automatism or blind impulsion, 'visible essences, spectres, etc.' required the 'much more appropriate medium of poetry'. Within the supernatural framework of *The Dynasts* he would show the human race 'as one great network or tissue which quivers in every part when one point is shaken, like a spider's web if touched'.[3] In this vast, palpitating web the true realities were to take the form of spirits, spectral figures, hitherto called abstractions. By the time this note was made in 1886 the conception of the great poem was complete. All that remained to do was to write it.

Preparations for the realisation of this vast project obviously involved something different from, and more than, the *Trumpet-Major* notebook. Instead of the paraphernalia of a rural society agog with the incursion of regiments and their commanders, military and political, and threatened by invasion by a tyrant on the other side of a narrow strip of sea, he had to set forth the panoply of 'Europe in the Throes' (which was at one stage his proposed title for the work) beneath the spectatorial commentary of a group of Phantom Intelligences. Not half a dozen local hearts and heads, and roughly the same number of historical personages headed by King George, but more than a hundred speaking characters of genuine historical existence, headed by King and Emperor, statesmen, generals, marshals, admirals, and captains, not to mention a thronging stage-army of soldiers and seamen, militia men and beacon-watchers, courtiers, lords and ladies of fashion, priests, doctors, heralds, aides-de-camp, Members of Parliament, the Lord Mayor and Corporation of London. Hardy was to find room even for Mrs Damer because she bore a Dorchester name, and for Sir Timothy Shelley because he was the father of a fellow poet he loved. No doubt it was gratifying to him to record personages of local name and fame, and to set scenes on the local heath. Of his 130 scenes, however, fewer than half-a-dozen are within the borders of

Wessex: at Weymouth, on the Ridgeway, on Egdon, and at Durnover (Fordington) Field. 'Ay; begin small, and so lead up to the greater', is the comment of the Spirit Sinister when the first scene opens on Ridgeway; 'It is a sound dramatic principle.' Similarly, as the great drama begins to wane after the Battle of the Nations, the scene appropriately shifts to Durnover Green, Casterbridge, where the natives are burning Bonaparte in effigy, perhaps somewhat prematurely for Waterloo is yet to come. We feel that Hardy cannot resist the firelight on 'the grey tower of Durnover Church hard by', a landmark which he could see from his windows at Max Gate less than a mile away.

In the Preface to *The Trumpet-Major* Hardy tells us that the material he had collected from the recollections of eye-witnesses would have filled a volume thrice the length of his novel. *The Trumpet-Major* notebook, too, contains a good deal that he did not use. Dr Clifford has shown how much of this material went into *The Dynasts,* and the difference in his use of it there. But, of course, he required far more and very different material now. He engaged in an extensive course of reading in formal works of history and biography, and collected a considerable library around him at Max Gate. Some volumes still remain in the Dorset County Museum at Dorchester, though many more were dispersed by sale after his death, a fact which is hardly to be deplored as it would be if Hardy had been a formal scholar or a professional historian. A cynical person once said of books of historical scholarship, and specially of theses written for the degree of Ph.D., 'It all comes out of the books they read, and goes into the books they write.' Hardy's dealings with the books he read were those of a poet, not of a historian or any other kind of accumulative scholar. He went to history to find what he wanted, not to discover what he should find. What he wanted was determined not simply by the nature of his subject but by the nature of his vision of that subject, which, in turn, was the product of his 'idiosyncratic mode of regard.' In order to make music, as Coleridge once said, it is not enough to purchase flutes, fiddles and horns. You must know how to play. In order to make your facts speak truth, he went on to say, you must know the truth which ought to be proved and was intended at all times. You must carry your rule ready-made if you wish to measure aright. Perhaps this is little more than to say, with Collingwood, that you must know what questions to ask, but this verges upon heresy for the academic historian.

The original manuscript of *The Dynasts* has a footnote which says, 'It is intended to give a list of the chief authorities at the end of the Third Part.' This intention was never carried out, and the omission was a touch of genius. Like the celebrated silence of the dog in the night-time, it speaks worlds. To have supplied a 'list of the chief authorities' would have been a betrayal of Hardy's intentions, reducing *The Dynasts* to the ranks of History, which is altogether a subaltern art to Poetry, if it is an art at all. There can be no 'authorities' for a poem, unless it is to descend to an informative verse-sequence like Erasmus Darwin's *The Botanic Garden,* or John Dyer's *The Fleece,* from which a man may learn botany and the various technical procedures for turning wool into cloth. The man who thought to learn History from *The Dynasts* would resemble the great Duke of Marlborough when he said, 'Shakespeare — the only History I ever read'. We cannot say precisely what historical works Hardy read, nor would it add or detract from the greatness of his achievement if we could. To trace this or that line of poetry to this or that line in a history book that we know, or suppose, him to have read is an exercise in textual criticism which can be valuable but may sink into mere pedantry.

All the same, as Coleridge said, an epic-poem cannot, must not, be all poetry. Both the poet and the reader get tired, and how is poetry to rise to great heights unless it also sinks on occasions, if not to great depths, at any rate to the mundane and the commonplace? Where would we be in *The Prelude* had Wordsworth not sunk now and again into such heavy interbreathings as

> My drift hath scarcely,
> I fear, been obvious . . .

or

> That portion of my story I shall leave
> There registered . . .

Where should we be in *The Dynasts* without the stretches of small print? As with insurance policies, it is important to read them. At least a third of the poem is in prose. If anyone cared to extract from it the passages which in another drama would be called 'scene-setting' he would have an excellent scenario of European events over some ten years. Some scenes consist entirely of description, dumb show and commentary by the Spirits, nearly all in small print. The battle of Vimiero (Part 2, Act II, Scene vii) consists solely of stage direction and dumb show. Scenes iv and v of the same Act, which concern Madrid and the open sea between England and the Spanish Peninsula, revel in dumb show and choric commentary in italics. Act IV, Scene ii; Act V, Scene v; Act VI, Scene i (all in Part 2) consist only of solid small print and italics.

Writing about *The Dynasts* to Sir Sydney Cockerell in 1913, Wilfrid Scawen Blunt reported that he had 'read it conscientiously through without finding anything at all in it which has any business to be called poetry except a little piece on the battle of Trafalgar imitated from Kipling.' Wondering why so great a prose-writer as Hardy should have 'wasted himself in this way' on 'ditchwater from start to finish', he describes *The Dynasts* as 'Alison's *History of Europe* done into very poor blank verse eked out with prose where the writer gets into difficulties with his lines.'[4]

Sir Archibald Alison's *History of Europe,* in ten volumes, began to appear in 1833 and was being published at the rate of one volume every eighteen months throughout Hardy's young days. When he began to think about the historical background of his grand drama it was the readiest and most natural book to turn to in English. When precisely he read it there is no way of discovering. He probably made use of it in a workaday fashion for a good many years. It certainly qualified for his comment on his Napoleonic reading — 'very long and not very good.' He appears to have read most in the later volumes, especially when he was composing the passages on the Russian campaign (Part 3, Act I), when he also makes use of Tolstoy's *War and Peace,* which he scarcely distinguishes from formal history. To speak of his having 'done' Alison's *History* into verse of any kind, let alone 'very poor blank verse', is complete nonsense. There certainly were some 'authorities' (notably parliamentary debates) that Hardy did turn into some inevitably wooden blank verse, but Alison was not among them. For one thing, as Wilfrid Scawen Blunt should have known, poetry is not made like that. For another, if Hardy was looking for someone's history to do into verse, Alison was the wrong man. As well imagine Bernard Shaw 'doing' one of the Early Fathers. Hardy was a radical in politics and an agnostic, to say the least. Sir Archibald Alison was a Tory and an anxious ally of Divine Providence, as became a judge and strike-breaker. He was intent upon showing in his *History* that 'the actors were overruled by an unseen power which rendered their vices and ambitions the means of vindicating the justice of the divine administration, asserting the final triumph of virtue over vice, and ultimately affecting the deliverance of mankind.' In other words, as Disraeli said of Mr Wordy, 'to prove that Providence was on the side of the Tories'. Is it possible to imagine anything more remote from the poet of the Immanent Will and its designs? As the Spirit of the Years was to protest,

> Nothing appears of shape to indicate
> That cognizance has marshalled things terrene, . . .
> Rather they show that, like a knitter drowsed,
> Whose fingers play in skilled unmindfulness,
> The Will has woven with an absent heed
> Since life first was; and ever will so weave.[5]

It is not necessary for a man to share the underlying philosophy of a historian in order to make use of his history. One might have supposed, however, that Hardy could have found historians less repellent of his own view of things than Sir Archibald. As indeed he did. There was Hazlitt's *Life of Napoleon Bonaparte,* in four volumes, on his shelves, a spirited work by a Liberal of the Keats—Shelley school which Hardy so greatly loved, but full of inaccuracies and hero-worship. There was also Sir Walter Scott's *The Life of Napoleon Bonaparte,* a work of the great novelist's later years, and also in many volumes, which Hardy never mentions.

His other stand-by, mercifully free of the Providential view
of things, but still twenty volumes of 500 pages each, was
Histoire du Consulat et de l'Empire by Adolphe Thiers. This
came out between 1845 and 1861, for there were giants in
the land in the days before the dictaphone and the
typewriter. Sir Archibald wore out his amanuensis and had to
write the final pages of his *History* with his own fair hand in
order to be in time for the anniversary of Waterloo, laying
down his pen at three o'clock of a fine June morning in
1842, but without recalling Gibbons' great moment by the
Lake of Lausanne more than fifty years before. As for M.
Thiers, he was too fast for the printers. Merely as a physical
feat, his *Histoire* is quite out of the ordinary. From all that
can be made out from examining the volumes Hardy had at
Max Gate — in addition to the Paris edition of 1857, he had a
translation by D. Forbes Campbell — and the manuscript of
The Dynasts, Hardy would appear to have known his Thiers
better than anything. It is significant that his poem, 'The
Peasant's Confession,' is prefaced by a quotation from Thiers.
No doubt he referred to him as 'M. Thiers', for the historian
was an active and celebrated figure in the politics of France
in Hardy's childhood and youth: twice Prime Minister under
King Louis-Philippe, and later President of the Third Repub-
lic. His *Histoire* must have stood in Hardy's study as a
monument to the great Provençal, and provincial, of illegitimate birth — to *la Carrière ouverte aux talents* in the
tradition of the Revolution. It was Adolphe Thiers who
brought Napoleon's remains back to Paris in state in the year
of Hardy's birth. Thiers upheld the memory of the Emperor
as the child and champion of the Revolution, the symbol of
enlightenment and progress. The greatness of the man is
never for a moment allowed to suffer question. Holding him
to be the greatest of historic men, Thiers applied himself
sagely to discovering the point at which, and the reasons for
which, so great a man should have taken the turning to defeat
and failure. Lamartine once said that Thiers was 'the
accomplice of fortune', or that he only censured Napoleon
for having ultimately failed. This is unfair, but it may be that
anyone whose admiration always triumphs over censure on
account of his affection must always give an impression of a

certain opportunism in his judgements. At any rate, Thiers'
Histoire with its unremitting enthusiasm for the 'ideal despot'
was the first to deal with its subject on a level appropriate to
its majesty and its historic greatness. Hardy's portrait falls far
short of the great exponent of the Napoleonic theme. There
is always something, indeed not a little, of the denigration
which had been common to the Wessex men who stood to
arms against the Corsican on their beloved soil. Perhaps
Edmund Blunden put his finger on this defect in his remark
that when Hardy spoke of Napoleon one always felt that 'the
unshaven jowl of the thwarted Corsican was just outside the
window'.[6] Perhaps he had been too near to him.

'My argument is that War makes rattling good history; but
Peace is poor reading', says the Spirit Sinister. 'So I back
Bonaparte for the reason that he will give pleasure to
posterity.'[7] Neither here, nor elsewhere, was Hardy cheapen-
ing Napoleon because of his career as a warmonger. Hardy
was a peaceable man, hating war and all forms of violence as
do most good soldiers. But he was no parlour pacifist. He
never carried a gun, even a game-gun, and it may be doubted
whether he ever heard a shot fired in anger, though he stood
on the balcony of Barrie's flat in the Adelphi one night in the
summer of 1917 to watch the searchlights during an air-raid.
He came from people who know, without having to discuss
the question, that you can't live in an island with any choice
of how you will live unless you are prepared finally to fight
for the privilege. And he valued the commonplace benefits of
civilisation, even if they were not the ultimate blessings in a
malign universe. He resented the limitations placed on the
will of man by his own nature and the physical frame of
existence, but — as Rebecca West once said — 'there never
was a great writer who more completely swallowed civilization, hook, line and sinker, than Thomas Hardy.' There was
indeed something distinctly brisk and military about his
carriage and bearing, and one soldier-poet has said that he
was of the stuff of which corps commanders are made. He
held Siegfried Sassoon and T.E. Lawrence among his dearest
friends. Younger men, men of action, soldiers, these were the
kind of men whose company he preferred. Talking of 'good

Conservatives and staunch Anglicans', Florence Hardy reports of him in his last years,

> T.H. declares that he understands that type of person better than any others, and he prefers to know the rather narrow churchy conservative county person to the brilliant young writer who is always popping in and out of the divorce-court.[8]

'Immensely peaceful as he was . . . his being still kindled at the hint of heroic contest', Edmund Blunden notes: 'even in his ninth decade he could flash out a reminder of the times when swords were bright in honour's cause; he could give a martial rhythm to a sleepy summer moment.'[9] Soldiers appear in his novels, his short stories and his poems, and the battle-pieces are some of the finest in *The Dynasts*. He will not glorify war, but neither will he shirk it as a necessary part of the story. His favourite military historian, Sir William Napier, was a professional soldier who taught that 'war is the rule of the world, and that from man to the smallest insect all living things are at strife', a fact of which Hardy was well aware even before he read Darwin, and about which he wrote the striking poem, 'In a Wood'. But he could see the sadness and suffering in the strife and this led to the greatness of poems like 'Drummer Hodge' in which Hardy's pity is strongly felt.

The general drama of pain to which this situation of universal conflict contributed distressed Thomas Hardy all his life, and especially in relation to the sufferings of animals. It seemed to him particularly illustrative of the injustice of things that dumb animals should suffer pain in consequence of courses in which they had no part or choice. These were the innocent creatures of that great poem, 'Afterwards':

> . . . He strove that such innocent creatures should come
> to no harm,
> But he could do little for them; and now he is gone. .

It was typical of Hardy not to leave it at that, but to provide money for their relief in his will. He was like Jude who picked his way on tiptoe among the earthworms and suffered grief when he saw trees cut down or lopped, 'from a fancy that it hurt them'. Like Jude, 'he was the sort of man who was born to ache a good deal . . . '[10]

Who but Hardy would have introduced the battle of Waterloo with a threnody upon the approaching terror and suffering of the rabbits, the moles, snails and earthworms crushed by the wheels of the cannon, the hoofs of horses, the 'terrible tread' of armed men?

> The snail draws in at the terrible tread,
> But in vain; he is crushed by the felloe-rim;
> The worm asks what can be overhead,
>
> And wriggles deep from a scene so grim,
> And guesses him safe; but he does not know
> What a foul red rain will be soaking him![11]

Who else but Hardy would remember the earthworms on the day of the dynasts? Who else would refrain from mentioning their office among the dead humans? To Hardy they are given remembrance for their own sake. The armies are intruders in the scene:

> The eyelids of eve fall together at last,
> And the forms so foreign to field and tree
> Lie down as though native, and slumber fast![12]

A poet who can write like that can be safely trusted to write of war.

Write of it he did, for it was the subject of *The Dynasts*, the Great Historical Calamity, or Clash of Peoples, which turned Europe into one vast battlefield for more than ten years ('The time covered by the action being about ten years' according to the author), and he read assiduously of it too. Not only Napier's *The History of the War in the Peninsula* and Ségur's *Napoléon et la Grande Armée en 1812*, Gleig's *The Leipzig Campaign* and *The Story of the Battle of Waterloo*, all formal works of military history, but William Beatty's *Authentic Narrative of the Death of Nelson* and the Baron Claude-Francois de Meneval's *Memoirs*, all of which embodied a measure of personal experience of the war as it was fought. They are the work of eye-witnesses, who were 'there', and always to be preferred by Hardy to the academic historian. Of course, he made regular use, as we have already seen, of C.H. Gifford's *History of the Wars*, his first history of the Napoleonic contest, since he read it in his father's house as a boy. As a result of self-immersion in such books over a number of years, along with even more years of talk with the old people of Wessex, he seems to have undergone a species of trauma not unlike that of the Prince Regent who, not long before Hardy was born, used to talk of his personal memories of the battle of Waterloo — at which he had not been present — much to the amusement of the Duke of Wellington. Hardy probably identified himself most readily with the deserters hiding in the cellars at Astorga, men of the English line-regiments tapping the casks of Spanish wine and wishing themselves

> at home in England again, where's there old-fashioned tipple, and a proper God A'mighty instead of this eternal 'Ooman and baby; — ay, at home a-leaning against old Bristol Bridge, and no questions asked, and the winter sun slanting friendly over Baldwin Street as 'a used to do![13]

Emotion recollected in tranquillity, no doubt. Like a good soldier Hardy was always hankering after tranquillity. His voice is surely to be heard among the Chorus of the Pities at the close of the bloody battle of Albuera with its splendid lyric:

> Hide their hacked bones, Earth! — deep, deep, deep,
> Where harmless worms caress and creep. —
> What man can grieve? what women weep?
> Better than waking is to sleep. Albuera![14]

9   Hardy and Napoleon

A present-day historian glancing down a list of the books Hardy read when preparing to write *The Dynasts* might be inclined to the impression that the poet had a liking for the second-rate, that he preferred the gossipy to the learned, and that he didn't much mind being 'out of date' or behind the times. Unkind critics have been heard to suggest that this is why he never provided his epic with a list of 'authorities'. These animadversions, however, lose both point and relevance when we recall that Hardy was not reading history in order to write it, and that what he wanted from his books was only what served his poetic purpose. What a historian regards as a second-rate book may serve the purposes of a poet better than a masterpiece. It is important, too, to remember the state of historical writing at the end of the nineteenth century. It was, to say the least, largely unprofessional, as it had remained throughout the century in Europe with the exception of Germany. That exclusive term, 'professional', as applied to the gentle art of history-writing, has only come into common use among educated people during the last fifty years or less. Hitherto, people who wrote history did so for other than academic or professional reasons. They did it because they took pleasure in history as a form of literature, as Gibbon and Macaulay did, or (at the lowest) as a form of propaganda. They were, in the proper usage of the word, 'amateurs'. Few of them, and scarcely one whose work has laid hold on the mind of posterity, wrote from, or for, a university.

What would Hardy have at his disposal today that he had not in the first decade of the present century? In the first place he would now have the fruits of the revolution in historical writing which have followed upon a total reorientation of outlook; a change which by the second half of the

wentieth century begins to appear retrospectively like a
landslip or a huge geological fault in the whole historical
landscape, and which is only now settling into a more or less
acceptable perspective. The enormity of the change is only to
be assessed by imagining a perspective from which the
gigantic figure of Karl Marx has been removed. Since 1935
the reader has beneath his eyes the fourteenth volume of
Halphen and Sagnac's *Peuples et Civilisations*. Entitled
'Napoléon', this volume deals with the history of the period
1799 — 1815 in terms of the new dispensation, and at once it
becomes plain to the reader from Georges Lefebvre's volume
that all previous histories — especially those Hardy read —
have lost a great deal of their relevance. The same impression
is to be derived from Albert Mathiez's popular *History of the
French Revolution,* an out-and-out Marxist interpretation
and the most authoritative left-wing interpretation since
Michelet. The nearest to what may be, indeed must be, called
the twentieth-century outlook which might have come within
Hardy's purview is the work of Albert Sorel. His great work
on Europe and the French Revolution began to appear in
1885, although it was not until the later volumes in 1903 and
1904 that the period most relevant to *The Dynasts* was
reached. It is in Sorel's fifth volume that he treats of
Napoleon in terms which Hardy would have been among the
first to understand, a figure who, but for the irresistible
current of history, would appear as nothing but 'a prodigious
and powerless individual'. He makes Napoleon acknowledge,
at the zenith of his power, 'I am the greatest slave among
men, my master has no entrails, and that master is the nature
of things . . . ' Of all the characters in his enormous cast,
Napoleon was the only one whom Hardy makes wholly
conscious of his subservience to the Immanent Will (though
he would have called it his Star).

> . . . Yet, 'tis true, I have ever known
> That such a Will I passively obeyed!

Although Hardy does not appear to have studied Sorel's great
work, he would have found much there to chime with his
imaginings. He would certainly have learned something from
the fifty pages of 'Étude critique sur *Bonaparte et le*

Directoire par M. Albert Sorel' by Raymond Guyot and Pierre Muret, which was published in the 'Revue d'Histoire Moderne et Contemporaine' for the years 1903-4.

The latest and most easily accessible work, however, was *The Life of Napoleon I* by an English historian, J. Holland Rose, which came out in 1901, the year before the first part of *The Dynasts* was written. Hardy undoubtedly possessed a copy of this work, which was to become the nearest and most obvious authority for English readers for many years. How early he may have acquired it, or precisely when — if ever — he read it, is likely to remain uncertain. It was probably sold when his library was dispersed after his death. The last record of it was in Messrs Commins' catalogue in 1966, where it was described as bearing the inscription, 'Thomas Hardy 1922'. He continued to acquire Napoleonic works even while he was composing his epic. The most interesting instance is P. Coquelle's *Napoléon et l'Angleterre, 1803-13* (Paris, 1904) which he read after writing Part 1. It was a grateful work for Hardy because of its concern with his predominant theme: the Napoleonic Wars as essentially a contest between Bonaparte and the English. He had emphasised in his Preface to *The Dynasts* that the slight regard shown by Continental writers to English influence and action throughout the contest had encouraged him to think there was room for a new handling of the theme 'which should re-embody the features of this influence in their true proportion'. As a patriot Hardy was proud of his country's part in the great contest, and a work like Coquelle's which concentrated on the war as a duel between Napoleon and England — the kingdom of Wessex enlarged — must have seemed to him to reach the heart of history. Chapter 12 was obviously studied by Hardy with special interest as it depicts Napoleon's growing hatred and jealousy of England and his meanness and vacillation.

It is rarely that one is able to trace a straightforward example of cause and effect between what Hardy read and what he wrote, but the effect of reading Coquelle's book is at once apparent in the first two scenes of Part 2 of *The Dynasts* which were written immediately after reading *Napoléon et l'Angleterre*. In the first of these he dramatises

the story of Charles James Fox, the British Foreign Secretary
in the Ministry of All-the-Talents, being tempted by a French
agent to patronise his offer to assassinate Napoleon. Fox
turns him out and consults his conscience about informing
the enemy:

> Now what does strict state-honour ask of me? —
> No less than that I bare this poppling plot
> To the French ruler and our fiercest foe!—[1]

The next scene consists entirely of antiphonal chanting by
Rumours to which the Spirits poised above the Channel listen
as couriers shoot 'shuttlewise to Paris and London, turn and
turn', conducting the argument between the old enemies.
'Fortunately for the manufacture of corpses,' as the Spirit
Sinister points out, 'Napoleon sticks to this veto, and so
wards off the awkward catastrophe of a general peace
descending upon Europe.'

Coquelle's book, however, is of far less importance for its
influence upon the substance and the language of the first
two scenes in Part 2 than for its part in strengthening Hardy's
conception of the War as a duel between Napoleon and the
English. The conception was there from the beginning, an old
Wessex notion, no doubt. Napoleon himself is made to voice
the personal animosity in Part 1, Act IV, Scene i. After
Trafalgar, when he is boasting that 'Ships can be wrecked by
land', Napoleon exclaims:

> 'Tis all a duel 'twixt this Pitt and me . . .

But with Parts 2 and 3 this theme waxes larger year by year.
In the sixth scene of Act I of Part 2, when Napoleon has
Prussia at his feet, the ladies of Berlin are heard discussing the
question, whose turn next? Russia? Austria? The fifth lady
says,

> Neither: England. — Yea,
> Her he still holds the master mischief-mind
> And marrer of the countries' quietude,
> By exercising untold tyranny
> Over all ports and seas.

To which the second lady retorts, 'Then England's doomed!'
But there follows at once a Chorus of Ironic Spirits with

aerial music, tantamount to the singing of 'Rule Britannia'. While Napoleon might deem himself omnipotent on the Continent, he was unlikely to 'warden the waves', for the weaving Will from eternity, hemming them in by a circling sea, evolved the fleet of the Englishry.

> This, O this is the cramp that grips!
> And freezes the Emperor's finger-tips
> From signing a peace with the Land of Ships.

It would be too much to say that this chorus is a paraphrase of Coquelle's prose, but it is little removed from the final chapter of his book. Napoleon's reply to the Spirit of the Years in his final words in the drama is as close. The Spirit of the Years has carefully excepted England from those who had, in Napoleon's day of glory, bent to his footstool, England

> Whose tough, enisled, self-centred, kindless craft
> Has tracked me, springed me, thumbed me by the throat,
> And made herself the means of mangling me![2]

In Coquelle, too, Hardy must have been gratified to find a French historian who made no bones about blaming Napoleon for the breach of the Peace of Amiens. Coquelle was not a university historian, as Hardy cannot have failed to notice. Like the patriot-poet he was not one to indulge in hair-splitting excuses for what ordinary people call plain lack of good faith.

Historians, even of the Liberal persuasion, are apt to fall under the spell of Napoleon. Herbert Fisher, within five years of the completion of *The Dynasts,* opened the short life of Napoleon which he wrote for the Home University Library with an evocation of the man's charm:

As we think of Napoleon Bonaparte what a world of visions and memories rises before the mind! Who does not know the outward form of the greatest conqueror and captain of modern times: the small, almost dwarfish, figure, the rounded symmetry of the head, the pale olive cheek and massive brow, the nose and lips carved as it were from the purest marble of the antique world; and above all the deep-set eyes of lustrous gray, now flashing with electric fires, now veiled in impenetrable contemplation?[3]

'I should think I did know Boney', says old Solomon Selby in 'A Tradition of 1804', when he recounts his sight of the fellow in the⁻ light of a dark lantern one night in 1804 in a Wessex cove.

> I should have known him by half the light o' the lantern. If I had seen a picture of his features once, I had seen it a hundred times. There was his bullet head, his short neck, his round yaller cheeks and chin, his gloomy face, and his great glowing eyes. He took off his hat to blow himself a bit, and there was the forelock in the middle of his forehead, as in all the draughts of him. In moving, his cloak fell a little open, and I could see for a moment his white-fronted jacket and one of his epaulets.[4]

In writing this passage, Hardy was no doubt recalling the 'hieroglyphic portrait' of the ogre which 'existed as a print down to the present day in an old woman's cottage near "Overcombe" ' according to his Preface to *The Trumpet-Major.*

When Hardy saw the Prince Napoleon at the funeral of the young Louis Napoleon at Chislehurst in 1879 he described him as of 'complexion dark, sallow, even sinister: a round projecting chin: countenance altogether extraordinarily remindful of Boney', and he later said it had been of 'enormous use to him, when writing *The Dynasts,* in imagining the Emperor's appearance'.[5] And he liked to tell how, according to William Barnes, one of his kinsmen had nearly come to blows with Louis Napoleon, then visiting friends in the neighbourhood, on a Sunday afternoon in the South Walk, Dorchester.

Being Thomas Hardy he could never resist the fascination of personal proximity to a great historical figure. We have already seen how he searched for the Bridge of Lodi and visited the battlefield at Waterloo. He conceived the scene of Napoleon's coronation in Milan Cathedral while sitting in the sun with his wife on the Cathedral roof, or so he thought likely. But, as with Beethoven, it was for the young Napoleon

alone, 'the child and champion of the Revolution', that he
was able to retain any enthusiasm. At the time of the
Volunteer Movement of 1859, when his countrymen thought
that they had reason to fear a recrudescence of the
Napoleonic threat to their shores from the great Emperor's
nephew, 'inheritor of an invading name', as Meredith called
him, Hardy was still living down in Dorset, training to be an
architect with John Hicks, and he seems to have been more
interested in Paedo-baptism than in patriotic preparations.
When the Second Empire fell in 1870, Hardy and Emma
Gifford were sitting in the garden of the Rectory at St Juliot
and reading Tennyson. And he records in the notebook that

> On the day that the bloody battle of Gravelotte was
> fought they [i.e. Emma and he] were reading Tennyson in
> the grounds of the rectory. It was at this time and spot
> that Hardy was struck by the incident of the old horse
> harrowing the arable field in the valley below, which, when
> in far later years it was recalled to him by a still bloodier
> war, he made into the little poem . . . entitled 'In Time of
> "the Breaking of Nations".'[6]

Reading Napoleonic history for professional purposes in the
'eighties', and after, he could not have helped noticing the
way French historians laid the blame for the catastrophe of
1870, indeed for the whole episode of 'Napoleon the Little',
upon the fatal persistence of the legend of Napoleon the
Great. Pierre Lanfrey's *Histoire de Napoléon,* began to come
out in 1869, even before Napoleon III fell. Hardy bought the
1876 edition for his library at Max Gate. It was a work
calculated to destroy any illusions he may ever have
entertained about the central figure of *The Dynasts.* Hardy's
copy of Lanfrey is still among his books in the Dorchester
Museum, and there is plenty of internal evidence of his use of
it, especially in composing the passages concerning Admiral
Villeneuve at, and after, Trafalgar in the fifth Act of Part 1.
The account given by the Recording Angels in the opening
scene is based closely upon passages in Lanfrey's second
volume where,

> Gloomy Villeneuve grows rash, and, darkly brave,
> Leaps to meet war, storm, Nelson — even the grave.[7]

Hardy shares Lanfrey's sympathy with the wretched man's suffering at the hands of his cruel taskmaster. Scene vi of this Act, where the defeated Admiral commits suicide at the Inn at Rennes, crying,

> Ungrateful master; generous foes; Farewell!

is wholly based on Lanfrey's account in the same volume, although, of course, the merciful words of the Spirit of the Pities,

> May his sad sunken soul merge into nought
> Meekly and gently as a breeze at eve!

are the poet's philosophically incongruous intervention. After Waterloo, one is happy to record, Hardy was able to allow the Spirit of the Pities even to check the Spirit Ironic in his comments on the fall of Bonaparte:

> Peace. His loaded heart
> Bears weight enough for one bruised, blistered while![8]

'A keen, searching north wind blows through Lanfrey's pages', wrote G. P. Gooch. The idol is swept contemptuously from its pedestal. After this, and after 'Taine's missile',[9] a reaction set in at the hands of Napoleon's worshippers, and it became impossible to know Napoleon as he really was until the last decade of the century. Hardy, however, seems to have stood by Lanfrey. Whether he ever read much in Masson, Vandal, Houssaye, or Arthur Levy, the rebuilders of the Legend, is more than doubtful. After all, Lanfrey was nearer to his own generation, and like most first-generation critics he felt no obligation to find ingenious excuses for the tyrant and the warmonger. Like the Englishmen who had fought him to a standstill, he could discover nothing in him but ambition and the lust for power, the enemy of liberty, the proponent of violence and trickery. The Spirit of the Years, who most often seems to speak for Hardy himself, addresses him in the last lines of the last scene:

> Worthless these kneadings of thy narrow thought,
> Napoleon; gone thy opportunity!
> Such men as thou, who wade across the world

> To make an epoch, bless, confuse, appal,
> Are in the elemental ages' chart
> Like meanest insects on obscurest leaves . . .

There is nothing here of the man who consolidated the Revolution, but only of the man who took away liberty, sought to destroy all independence of mind, and created a new nobility of military adventurers who served him in sterile wars which brought the catastrophes of 1812-15.

To the understanding of Napoleon the poet of *The Dynasts* contributes nothing', wrote John Bailey. In fact, he tends to make him unintelligible because the whole conception of *The Dynasts* requires him to be a puppet, and a puppet can scarcely be saddled with moral responsibility, though Hardy plainly cannot bring himself to relieve him of all blame. His dilemma is inherent in any attempt to make a tragedy out of characters who have been robbed of moral choice. How real his dilemma is can be seen at the end of Part 3, Act VI, Scene iii, when the sleeping Emperor, in a scene reminiscent of that in Shakespeare's *Richard III* where the tyrant is visited by the ghosts of his victims on the night before Bosworth, is shown a puppet-scene under the showmanship of the Duke of Enghien. 'A little moral panorama would do him no harm,' as the Spirit Ironic says. As Napoleon gazes upon the skeletons rising from his various battlefields, he protests,

> Why, why should this reproach be dealt me now?
> Why hold me my own master, if I be
> Ruled by the pitiless Planet of Destiny?

Hardy is, of course, well enough aware that great tragedy can never be made out of automatism. Two of the principal conditions of tragedy are present: that it shall befall someone in an exalted station and that the calamity shall be of an exceptional character, but the third — that the principal character shall have taken part in bringing it about — is imperfectly realised. With Hardy, tragedy is imposed from without, not simply from defects in the protagonist, but inflicted upon him.[10] That he was aware of this can be seen in the final words of the Fore Scene, before the drama begins. 'Deem yet man's deeds self-done', says the Spirit of the Years, who, as we have already said, generally utters the sentiments of Hardy. It is as if he says, with a wink perhaps, 'for the sake of the play, we must allow men's deeds to appear self-done — just for the moment.' He had already quoted, with obvious relief, Coleridge's famous words about the 'willing suspension of disbelief for the moment, which constitutes poetic faith'. This is undoubtedly a flaw in the whole work, and it will only cease to disturb us when we tell ourselves that Hardy's concern was not to advance *The Dynasts* as a system of thought but as a poem. The only 'real' characters are the Spirits, who are outside, or above, the drama. They enable Hardy to get outside the world where the Immanent Will weaves its designs, its 'eternal artistries in Circumstance'. Their vision of the world, and of worlds beyond the world, and of the life that strives and suffers in them, is what imparts to *The Dynasts* its surpassing greatness.

Nor can we doubt that of all the characters in the drama the only one who could have read, and appreciated, *The Dynasts* is Napoleon, though he would undoubtedly have complained of the way he is treated therein. Hardy is rarely disloyal to history but he was prepared to paint a portrait all in black of Napoleon, which is something he would not have done in a work of fiction. It would have been inconsistent with his conception of Napoleon's inhumanity to portray him as suffering remorse or regret over his divorce from Josephine although there is plenty of historical evidence that he suffered in his feelings in carrying through this harsh act of state. Thiers provided more than a hint of it. Lanfrey's work contained a good deal of evidence. In it we read of Napoleon's talk of Charlemagne and of his interviews with Josephine at Fontainebleau and the truly Bourbon setting of his marriage to Marie Louise. Meneval, too, underlines Napoleon's real love of Josephine and the agony of his decision to become a Dynast. But Hardy pressed on with his portrait of politic ruthlessness, and the poetry at this point betrays for a moment by its failure his own emotional failure. Napoleon tells the weeping Josephine,

> My mind must bend
> To other things than out domestic pettings:
> The Empire orbs above our happiness,
> And 'tis the Empire dictates this divorce . . . [11].

Hardy was prepared to bend history to the purposes of his art, and he seems to have thought one of those purposes was to blacken the character of Napoleon even beyond the bounds of historical evidence. It was a mistake. It may help to account for the unfavourable view of another Dynast. Calling on his patient one October day in 1953, Lord Moran found him in bed, 'reading Hardy's *The Dynasts;* as far as he had got he did not like it.' His patient was Sir Winston Churchill.[12]

10　The Anti-Heroes

Like *Vanity Fair, The Dynasts* is a novel without a hero. 'I never took long with them,' Hardy said when talking to Virginia Woolf about his novels. 'The longest was *The Dinnasts* (so pronounced).'[1] It is thus that we have the author's own licence to include it among his novels. A novel, according to the Oxford Dictionary, is 'a fictitious prose narrative of sufficient length to fill one or more volumes, portraying character and actions of real life in a continuous plot . . .' 'Une fiction en prose d'une certaine étendue', says M. Abel Chevalley. Mr E. M. Forster finds a sense in which *The Dynasts* is more successful than the novels:

> Hardy's success in *The Dynasts* . . . is complete, there the hammer strokes are heard, cause and effect enchain the characters despite their struggles, complete contact between the actors and the plot is established.[2]

Although the same superb and terrible machine works in both, in the novels it never catches humanity in its teeth. In *The Dynasts* it does. That is why it is more successful.

When the hammer strokes are heard, when cause and effect enchain the characters despite their struggles, there can be no tragedy, only catastrophe, there can be no heroes or villains, only victims. In such a novel there can be no heroes. If there is a chief character it is Napoleon, and in an early note Hardy thought that the work might be called *Napoleon* or *Josephine,* or some other person's name. He does not appear to have thought of calling it *The Wellingtoniad,* the name which Macaulay imagined would be given the great epic of the Napoleonic Wars in the twenty-ninth century. Nor, despite the Englishness of his conception as it developed in his mind, did Hardy ever think of calling it after either of Napoleon's great opposite numbers, Nelson and Pitt. The chief character is a collective person — 'poor mankind', or rather that part of collective mankind which we call 'Europe'. 'Mock on, Shade, if thou wilt!' says the Spirit of the Pities as he closes up the first scene of Act III of Part 2. 'But others find/Poesy ever lurk where pit-pats poor mankind!' In the Fore Scene we see the Continent of Europe disclosed as,

> a prone and emaciated figure, the Alps shaping like a backbone, and the branching mountain-chains like ribs, the peninsular plateau of Spain forming a head . . . exhibiting as one organism the anatomy of life and movement in all humanity and vitalized matter . . .

When the drama is over, the After Scene exhibits a Europe which

> has now sunk netherward to its far-off position as in the Fore Scene, and it is beheld again as a prone and emaciated figure of which the Alps form the vertebrae, and the branching mountain-chains the ribs, the Spanish Peninsula shaping the head of the écorche. The lowlands look like a grey-green garment half-thrown off, and the sea around like a disturbed bed on which the figure lies.

While Europe may be called the scene of the drama, it is also its subject; not its hero, but its principal character.

Nevertheless, Hardy must have his heroes, even if we are to call them anti-heroes. He cannot resist giving a certain heroic dimension to such puppets as Nelson, Pitt and George III. The best of their puppetry is discovered in a certain equality which in the nature of things must subsist among victims. Nelson and Pitt suffer and die. George III goes mad, Hardy, of course, knowing nothing of porphyria. The Spirits — generally the Spirit of the Pities — see to it that a note of heroic valediction is sounded at their departure. The Pities chant as Nelson dies,

> His thread was cut too slowly! When he fell,
>   And bade his fame farewell,
> He might have passed, and shunned his long-drawn pain,
>   Endured in vain, in vain![3]

When William Pitt lies dead, the Spirit of the Years will not disturb his peace:

> Nay, I have spoke too often! Time and time,
> When all Earth's light has lain on the nether side,
> And yapping midnight winds have leapt on roofs,
> And raised for him an evil harlequinade
> Of national disasters in long train,
> That tortured him with harrowing grimace,
> Have I communed with that intelligence.
> Now I would leave him to pass out in peace,
> And seek the silence unperturbedly.[4]

And as the poor mad King draws nearer his end, the Spirit of the Pities wishes a God to pray to:

> Something within me aches to pray
> To some Great Heart, to take away
> This evil day, this evil day![5]

As if to sustain Hardy's notion of modern history, indeed modern life in general, as populated by automata and ghosts, the chief characters in the English scene at this time are noted for their somewhat poker-like rigidity, physically and temperamentally. This is particularly true of Pitt and Wellington, while George III seems to have had something of the jerky manners of a ventriloquist's doll. The one outstanding exception was Nelson. While there is something marionettish about his melodramatic action and temperament throughout his career, Nelson pre-empted the most moving scenes in the drama and some of Hardy's finest poetry. Masterly in construction, artistic unity and emotional force, Act V of Part 1 is Hardy's supreme achievement. It reflects the complete self-identification of the poet with his theme. Although chronologically Trafalgar comes early in the story it marks its emotional climax. This, we feel, is why *The Dynasts* was written. It reflects Hardy's reasons, as outlined in the Preface, for his concern with his subject: the proximity of Captain Hardy's old home under Blackdown, the role of the Wessex man as Nelson's flag-captain at Trafalgar, the central event of the contest, the victory which Napoleon could never forgive and from which he was never to recover, the role of Nelson himself as the great national hero. However, he did not try to steal Nelson from Norfolk. He had to be content with the other Hardy. Tess, it has been said, conveys the feeling that she is greater than destiny. Nelson, a historical character, was greater than fate, perhaps because, unlike Tess, the 'pure woman', he was aware of it, with his sense of his imminent fate in the last months of his life. He had been looking it in the eye for years and so was unafraid of it, indeed needed it in order to realise his idea of himself. At first sight he seems hardly fitted to be a Hardy character. One might imagine that, since he has overcome fate, he will cease to be interesting. Indeed Hardy does leave him to a purely historical course for a long time. Only for a brief moment do the Spirits enter into his story. Having launched him into it at the time of Napoleon's coronation at Milan ('I'll call in Nelson,' says the Spirit of the Years peremptorily), the Spirit is merely entrusted with the office of whispering in his ear, after which Nelson tells Collingwood that he has had 'warnings' that he has not long to live, and that he feels acutely conscious of public censure on his private life. After that he has only to win Trafalgar and die a hero's death. But the all-conquering Nelson conquers Thomas Hardy too, which was perhaps his greatest victory. Not even Hardy could turn Nelson completely into a puppet. Was this what Leslie Stephen had meant when he told the novelist years before that a historical character in a novel is almost always a nuisance? Certainly this historical character queers the pitch of the Immanent Will. That fell character, seen alongside Nelson, seems to fade into insignificance if not into irrelevance. Nelson himself, of course, would have said that this was because he believed in a still more potent character — Almighty God, 'the Great God whom I adore'. The poet had no opportunity to bring Nelson's celebrated Prayer before battle, with its closing petition that 'humanity after victory' should be 'the predominant feature of the British Fleet', but he brings in the spirit of it a thousand times more effectively by making Nelson say, when one of his men picked off the marksman who had fired the fatal shot,

> 'Twas not worth while! — He was, no doubt, a man
> Who in simplicity and sheer good faith

> Strove but to serve his country. Rest be to him!
> And may his wife, his friends, his little ones,
> If such he had, be tided through their loss,
> And soothed amid the sorrow brought by me.[6]

Time and again in the splendid Trafalgar scenes, Hardy achieves things that only Shakespeare can achieve. It is impossible to refrain from quoting the last conversation between Nelson and Hardy, when in reply to Nelson's question at the climax of the battle, 'What are you thinking, that you speak no word?', Captain Hardy says,

> Thoughts all confused, my lord: — their needs on deck,
> Your own sad state, and your unrivalled past;
> Mixed up with flashes of old things afar —
> Old childish things at home, down Wessex way,
> In the snug village under Blackdon Hill
> Where I was born. The tumbling stream, the garden,
> The placid look of the grey dial there,
> Marking unconsciously this bloody hour,
> And the red apples on my father's trees,
> Just now full ripe.[7]

What matter the religious, or unreligious, beliefs of a poet who could write like that?

In his detailed analysis of Act V, Dr W. R. Rutland has shown the sources whence Hardy may have taken many of the details of the Trafalgar scenes.[8] Of course, some of this tracking down of specific images or even facts to the texts of works Hardy read is a work of supererogation. When he speaks of the 'red-frothed' waves it is hardly necessary to suggest that he was remembering Joseph Mery's *Trafalgar* with its reference to corpses rolling about 'dans une écume rouge'. Nor do we need to learn that Sir Archibald Alison had described the morning sun shining full upon the sails of the combined fleets as they put out from Cadiz. Hardy goes one better than anything he may have read when he speaks of their shining in the sun's rays like satin, and more than one better when he speaks of the British Fleet sailing into sight:

> Where Nelson's hulls are rising from the west,
>   Silently.
> Each linen wing outspread . . . [9]

No doubt Thiers,[10] Alison,[11] Lanfrey[12] were all laid under contribution, while the main lines of tactics and fleet-movements throughout are taken from Edward Pelham Brenton's *The Naval History of Great Britain, 1783-1836.* And for Napoleon's plans for the conquest of England he had J. B. Capefigue's *L'Europe pendant le Consulat et L'Empire.*

Hardy's preference for the records of eye-witnesses and for people who had access to first-hand evidence is shown particularly in his writing of the Trafalgar scenes because he was concerned mostly with the last events of Nelson's life on board the *Victory,* and for those scenes he had the invaluable work of William Beatty, surgeon of the flagship, *Authentic.* Beatty's *Narrative of the Death of Lord Nelson* was published in 1807 and became the source upon which all other accounts are ultimately based. No other death of a hero has ever been recorded in such first-hand substantial detail as this. Hardy could have derived almost every detail from Robert Southey's *Life of Nelson* which was published in 1813, but a number of references to the members of the crew could have been taken only from Beatty's narrative, which is the sole source also of the detail concerning the preservation of the hero's body in spirit, something of which Hardy made grotesque, and very Hardyan, use in the story of how the *Victory's* crew 'broached the Adm'l' on the journey back to England. The magnificent song which brings Act V to a conclusion, 'The Night of Trafalgar', is Hardy's own. Here again, in these final touches, we are back in Wessex, and the truth is vouched for by Bob Loveday of Overcombe, 'one of the "Victory" men that's going to walk in the funeral.' The Immanent Will doesn't get a look-in when there are local hearts and heads on hand. Even Bob Southey stood a better chance, he having been born at Bristol, which is in outer Wessex. It was the merest chance that his sailor brother, Tom, fought at Copenhagen instead of Trafalgar. Robert recruited Tom while writing his *Life of Nelson* and asked his lieutenant brother for all the vivid and memorable details he could supply:

> You used to speak of the dead lying in shoal water at Copenhagen; there was the boatswain's mate or some-

body . . . Tell me about your guns . . . I walk among sea
terms as a cat does in a china pantry . . . [13]

Sir Geoffrey Callender's edition of Southey's book,
published in 1922, shows that Southey's fears of his own
inadequacy as (the words are his own) 'such a sad lubber'
were far from imaginary, though Sir Geoffrey acknowledged
handsomely the genius of the biography as portraiture.
Hardy's ancillary sources in Pelham Brenton's *Naval History*
and other technical works preserved him from the lubber's
errors. Hardly ever did he jeopardise his accuracy by
dependence on only one authority. How soundly he was
grounded as a scholar can best be seen from his use without
disaster of Joseph Mery's *Trafalgar*, for the most part a
frankly imaginative work, indeed a novel. What doubtless
attracted Hardy to Mery was the fact that his book was
dedicated to Villeneuve's standard-bearer *(garde-aigle)* on his
flagship at Trafalgar, one Donnadieu.

The portrait of Pitt is rounded off in Scene v of Act V
which immediately follows the death of Nelson and where
the Prime Minister attends the Lord Mayor's banquet. This
has the Shakespearian touch with its First, Second, Third and
Fourth Citizens in the cheering crowd in Cheapside. Standing
where it does, between Nelson's death and Villeneuve's
suicide, it brings a breath of humour between passages of
tragic grandeur and of woe. The spectator who opens and
shuts his lips without uttering a sound ('It's a very mean
practice of ye to husband yourself at such a time, and gape in
dumbshow like a frog in Plaistow Marshes', says his neighbour) on the grounds that someone must save something in
these days of high taxation if the country isn't to be
bankrupt as Mr Pitt himself; and the boy who 'don't like
Billy' (Pitt) because he killed Uncle John's parrot by pressing
Uncle John for the Navy, so that his parrot talked itself to
death; and the very language in which such humour is
couched ('You had better have a care of this boy, friend. His
brain is too precious for the common risks of Cheapside.'): it
is all superbly comic, and yet full of meaning, as we see when
Hardy contrives to bring in quite unaffectedly one of the
great historical truths of the time — 'the French papers say

that our loss in him is greater than our gain in ships; so that
logically the victory is theirs.' By the juxtaposition of the
'great' and the 'little', of historical event contrasted with the
little lives of men, Hardy puts history into a perspective and
gives us his vision of war's annals clouding into night 'Ere
their story die'.

Not least to be admired in this scene of the Citizens
watching the 'great' is the felicity with which Hardy puts
Pitt's famous Guildhall speech into that mixture of poetry
and prose which is peculiarly his own. 'Those words of this
man Pitt' do indeed 'ring tonight/In their first mintage to the
feasters here', and Hardy avoids the danger of over-quotation
by making us feel it to be true that,

> . . . words were never winged with apter grace,
> Or blent with happier choice of time and place,
> To hold the imagination of this strenuous race.[14]

When in the next Act the Prime Minister, at the news of
Austerlitz, asks, 'Is there a map of Europe handy here?' we
fear the obvious. It might have been better to leave it at Pitt's
query on reading the dispatch, 'Where's Austerlitz?' We may
be certain, however, that questioned on the point Hardy
would have made the simple retort, 'But he did say it, didn't
he?' Two scenes later, when the dying man is heard to moan,
'My country! How I leave my country!', Hardy uses one of
the attributed last sayings of Pitt, but he tactfully omits
another: 'I think I could eat one of Bellamy's veal pies.'
Coleridge never said a less true thing than when he said, 'Not
a sentence of Mr Pitt's has ever been quoted.' However, he
said that in 1800 — five years too early.

The portrait of George III is the most successful of the
Dynasts, for the 'good old King' appears to have had all the
characteristics of a puppet, with his staccato manner of
speech, his 'Hey, what?' and his 'what-what-what?' Hardy
brings out all the strange juxtaposition of the patriot-king's
pride in his royalty and his heedless obstinacy. On the one
hand he will

> read it as a thing
> of signal augury, and one which bodes
> Heaven's confidence in me and in my line,
> That I should rule as King in such an age![15]

and on the other will not think of lightening Pitt's burden by admitting Fox and Grenville and their friends to share his responsibilities:

> Believe me, Pitt, you underrate yourself;
> You do not need such aid . . .
> Rather than Fox, why, give me civil war![16]

He killed Billy Pitt as certainly as Billy Pitt killed Uncle John's parrot. 'The name of his disease is — Austerlitz!', says the Bishop of Lincoln at his death-bed. 'And yet he might have borne it', says the physician,

> had the weight
> Of governmental shackles been unclasped,
> Even partly, from his limbs last Lammastide,
> When that despairing journey to the King
> At Gloucester Lodge by Wessex shore was made
> To beg such. But relief the King refused . . .
> The fibre that would rather snap than shrink
> Held out no longer. Now the upshot nears.[17]

Yet for all the King's fatal obstinacy, Hardy makes it clear that George III's personal qualities contributed much to England's survival — and her victory. Never for one moment, by way of contrast to the great majority of writers, does Hardy permit himself a suspicion of a sneer at the 'very obstinate and comical old gentleman' who would persist in sailing in Weymouth Bay at peril of being kidnapped by the French.

'What curious structure do I see outside, sir?' Pitt asks as he looks out of the window of Gloucester Lodge, wondering at the make-shift structure on the Esplanade. It's but a stage, a type of all the world', the King tells him, a stage on which the burgesses have arranged for there to be combats at single-stick, and on which, afterwards, there will be a grinning match through horse-collars. The King describes it as 'a very humorous sport which I must stay here and witness; for I am interested in whatever entertains my subjects.' To this the weary Minister can only remark, 'Not one in all the land but knows it, sir.'[18]

When the King's malady advances upon him and his

doctors threaten him with a strait-jacket, he recalls these happy days by the Wessex shore and pleads for gentler treatment by virtue of his earlier conduct:

> I do assure you truly, my good friends,
> That I have done no harm! In sunnier years
> Ere I was throneless, withered to a shade,
> Deprived of my divine authority —
> When I was hale, and ruled the English land —
> I ever did my utmost to promote
> The welfare of my people, body and soul! . . .
> I am most truly sorry, gentlemen,
> If I have used language that would seem to show
> Discourtesy to you for your good help
> In this unhappy malady of mine . . .
> A king should bear him kingly; I, of all,
> One of so long a line. O shame on me![19]

Hardy wrings our hearts for this, the least and sorriest of the dynasts, as for another Lear.

Beside the King, Wellington is a mere stick. Hardy was a boy of twelve when the great Duke had been buried to an Empire's lamentation, as Tennyson described it in his great 'Ode', and no doubt the Grand Old Man was one of the more magnificent trappings of that civilization which Hardy was supposed to have 'swallowed' so completely. He makes us see Wellington in *The Dynasts,* riding through Brussels on the way to the field of Waterloo 'in a grey frock-coat and small cocked hat, frigid and undemonstrative', or greeting Marshal Blucher at Ligny 'deliberate, judicial, almost indifferent'. The girl whose sweetheart rides behind him turns from the window in tears: 'I don't want to see him. I don't want to see anything any more!' On the field of Waterloo itself he is to be seen through the cannon-smoke, 'on his bay charger Copenhagen, in light pantaloons, a small plumeless cocked hat, and a blue cloak which shows its white lining when blown back.' All the views we get of the Duke are pictures from a scrap-book, familiar sights in every cottage of Victorian England. The Duke rides the whirlwind and controls the storm. He says all the right things: 'Hard pounding this, my men! I truly trust/You'll pound the longest (this to the British squares), and 'Stand up, Guards!' (to Maitland's two thousand as they finally stem the Old Guard in their last assault). He even has time to rejoin, 'By God, and have you!' to Uxbridge's cry, 'I have lost my leg, by God!' Unfortunately, *The Dynasts* ends when 'The reds disappear from the sky and the dusk grows deeper', and there is no opportunity to report Mr Creevey's record of the Duke's summing-up, when he said it had been 'a damned nice thing — the nearest run thing you ever saw in your life', and 'By God! I don't think it would have done if I had not been there.'

Where the Duke comes to life is in the Peninsula scenes, before he became 'The Duke'. Arthur Wellesley first appears swearing, at Salamanca, and he comes to life when he hears that Colonel Dalbiac's wife had ridden in the charge behind her husband. He responds to this as Hardy himself would have responded, because he knows the lady for a Wessex woman;

> Why that must be Susanna, whom I know —
> A Wessex woman, blithe, and somewhat fair . . .

But he at once remembers discipline, and comments Hardy-like,

> Not but that great irregularities
> Arise from such exploits.

As for the widow of 'Prescott of the Seventh' hunting for her husband's body on the field in the dusk,

> Well, I'm damned sorry for her. Though I wish
> The women-folk would keep them to the rear:
> Much awkwardness attends their pottering round![20]

The female camp-followers are worse than the officers' wives. As Joseph Bonaparte, driving away after his defeat at Vitoria, is made to comment:

> The bare unblinking truth hereon is this:
> The Englishry are a pursuing army,
> And we a flying brothel! See our men —
> They leave their guns to save their mistresses![21]

When a load of these ladies appears on the scene, Wellington
orders them to be packed off to Pamplona:

> We've neither list nor leisure for their charms.
> By God, I never saw so many who——s
> In all my life before![22]

This, like everything in the Peninsula scenes, is all very true
and human. Hardy in Spain is never far from home. Not only
does he bring to life the Duke and the Marshals, Sir John
Moore, the King of Spain and the Queen and her lover, but
he puts on record the Unknown Soldier.

In one sense Drummer Hodge in Hardy's poem of that
name is an Unknown Soldier, as his generic name indicates.
And another Unknown Soldier was that 'mouldering soldier
. . . your countryman' whose humble grave Hardy was to
commemorate in another poem written at the time of the
South Africa War.[23] But it is in *The Dynasts,* years before the
twentieth-century cult of the Unknown Soldier, that Hardy
paid his greatest tribute to these unknown soldiers. The cast
of *The Dynasts* records Samuel Clark, officer's servant who
lies buried at West Stafford in Dorset, and Thomas Young of
Sturminster Newton who fought at Vitoria, Toulouse and
Waterloo. Like Shakespeare's yeomen under the orchard-trees
on the night before Agincourt, these men gain a tongue and a
certain immortality. 'I wonder', says Sergeant Young, 'I
wonder how Stourcastle is looking this summer night, and all
the old folks there!', and he entertains the hussars at the
camp-fire of Vitoria with his rendering of 'Budmouth Dears':

> When we lay where Budmouth beach is,
> O, the girls were fresh as peaches,
> With their tall and tossing figures and their eyes of
> blue and brown . . . [24]

Hardy's loving record of these obscure lives which he
preserves among those of the Captains and the Kings, and his
gentle regard for all that is native, faithful and enduring, gives
his work its noblest and most distinctive character.

11   Collectives, Crowds, Caterpillars

The human race to be shown as one great network or tissue which quivers in every part when one point is shaken, like a spider's web if touched.

Hardy's note on the projected drama, 1886[1]

In *The Dynasts* European mankind at war is seen as a collective, and from their lofty viewpoint in the Overworld the attendant Spirits describe the spectacle constantly in terms of vermicular or thread-like shapes which creep or shuffle their length along. The Spirit of the Pities, viewing Napoleon's *Grande Armée* in retreat from Moscow, speaks of

> An object like a dun-piled caterpillar
> Shuffling its length in painful heaves along,
> Hitherward . . . . Yea, what is this Thing we see
> Which, moving as a single monster might,
> Is yet not one but many?[2]

While the Spirits cannot agree whether they are looking at a terrestrial tragedy or comedy, they agree that the thing they are looking at is 'one organism'.

What happens to individuals when they are merged in the collective, especially under the stress of battle, amounts to a certain dehumanisation. When the collective is struck by fear or panic, its component members become stupefied, mechanical automata. Men in a defeated army seem to move like somnambulists. At all times such people are likely to fall below normal standards of behaviour.

The beast-like character of mobs has been a commonplace ever since Plato called the People, collectively, 'the great beast'. In Shakespeare, people in the mass are seen as 'the blunt monster with uncounted heads', 'the rabblement' and

'The beast with many heads'. Burke called them 'the swinish multitude'. The action of 'the people' in the French Revolution on such occasions as the taking of the Bastille and the September Massacres, not to mention the mobs of the Gordon riots a few years earlier, created a trauma among property-owners for years to come. Burke, who seems to have been driven mad, could describe the French Revolution as a frightful and formless monster emerging from the tomb of the murdered monarchy. Coleridge, who was in many ways his disciple, spoke of *vox populi* as equally likely to be *vox diaboli,* a case of demoniac obsession. During the first half of the nineteenth century this fear and horror of 'the mob' was powerful in England, and Thomas Hardy grew up in the aftermath. The historians whose work he read wrote often of armies in terms of monstrosity. Alison wrote of the Allied forces entering Leipzig 'like a huge monster, bleeding at every pore, but still unsubdued', while Capefigue likened the army in retreat from Moscow to the corpse of a giant falling into putrefaction. Napier's *Peninsula War* speaks of the armies at Salamanca, where he was present, 'coiling and winding like angry serpents', a similitude which Alison likewise employs for the French columns at Waterloo, likening them to 'huge serpents clad in glittering scales'. Such images might come readily to anyone writing of marching armies, and especially in an age when soldiers were

> Accoutred in kaleidoscopic hues
> That would persuade us war has beauty in it!

The rainbow-passage which begins, 'Behold the gorgeous coming of those horse' in Part 3 (Act VII, Scene iv) is given to the Spirit of the Pities, but the Spirit does end by describing these gorgeous colours as

> A lingering-on till late in Christendom,
> Of the barbaric trick to terrorize
> The foe by aspect!

But it is plain from the Waterloo scenes that Hardy agreed with the Spirit Sinister's remark of long before that 'War makes rattling good history'.

As Dr Emma Clifford, who has assembled a number of

these images from Hardy's reading, has wisely reminded us,
there is no need to suppose that the sources necessarily exert
any great influence on *The Dynasts,* but it is at any rate plain
that the poet was by no means always at odds with them
even in his most imaginative writings.[3] Hardy, a Londoner for
so many years of his middle life, needed no literary
prompting in order to perceive something monstrous, even
horrific, about crowds. The man who had lain down in
boyhood among the shepherds and ploughmen in quiet
country places sometimes found it hard to sleep when as a
man he lay down in Upper Tooting. He experienced a certain
'horror at lying down in close proximity to "a monster whose
body had four million heads and eight million eyes" '. He
would look out of his bedroom like Professor Teufelsdröckh
in his high watchtower. When the air was clear he could see a
long way across London. He enters one such occasion in his
journals in 1880:

> In upper back bedroom at daybreak: just past three. A
> golden light behind the horizon; within it are the Four
> Millions. The roofs are damp gray: the streets are still filled
> with night as with a dark stagnant flood whose surface
> brims to the tops of the houses. Above the air is light. A
> fire or two glares within the mass. Behind are the Highgate
> Hills. On the Crystal Palace hills in the other direction a
> lamp is still burning up in the daylight. The lamps are also
> still flickering in the street, and one policeman walks down
> it as if it were noon.[4]

It was, he thought, 'The fiendish precision or mechanism of
town-life' that made it so intolerable to the sick and infirm.

> London appears not to *see itself.* Each individual is
> conscious of *himself,* but nobody conscious of themselves
> collectively . . . There is no consciousness here of where
> anything comes from or goes to — only that it is present.[5]

At Piccadilly Circus he observes 'the kiln-dried features
around.' At Marble Arch, in the roar of London he asks,

> What is it composed of? . . . Some wear jewels and
> feathers, some wear rags. All are caged birds; the only

difference lies in the size of the cage. This too is part of the tragedy.[6]

But Hardy made his most striking note on the crowd-monster after looking down from a high window on Ludgate Hill to see the Lord Mayor's Show. Mrs Hardy said that the surface of the crowd reminded her of a cauldron of boiling porridge. Hardy himself saw it as, 'a creature whose voice exudes from its scaly coat and who has an eye in every pore of its body'. As the crowd grows denser, he notes that

> it loses its character of an aggregate of countless units, and becomes an organic whole, a molluscous black creature having nothing in common with humanity, that takes the shape of the streets along which it has lain itself, and throws out horrid excrescences and limbs into neighbouring alleys.[7]

In *The Dynasts* it becomes,

> . . . an unnatural Monster, loosely jointed,
> With an Apocalyptic Being's shape,
> And limbs and eyes a hundred thousand strong,
> And fifty thousand heads; which coils itself
> About the buildings there.[8]

The Spirit of the Years calls this fearful creature, composed of the Prussians at Ligny, 'The Monster Devastation'. •

Hardy never speaks of the Collectives, whether mobs or armies, with the terror of a Tory historian like Alison. Nor does he view them with the fascinated contempt of the modern sociologist or the student of Group Psychology. He simply makes us realise that such groups are never less than a composite of human flesh and blood. 'They are shapes that bleed, mere mannikins or no', says the Spirit of the Pities, who speaks unmistakably with the voice of Hardy himself, as he reproaches the Spirit of the Years with 'small sense of mercy'. Each of these mannikins 'has parcel in the total Will'. They are 'Limbs of Itself' even if the whole 'overrides them as a whole its parts'. The Spirit of the Pities, indeed, cannot refrain from regret that the sad story must be told at all.

> . . . 'twere better far
> Such deeds were nulled, and this strange man's career
> Wound up, as making inharmonious jars
> In her creation whose meek wraith we know.
> The more that he, turned man of mere traditions,
> Now profits naught.[9]

Napoleon's 'larger potencies' — for example, 'To throne fair Liberty in Privilege room' — have become tainted by his ambitions and sunk to common plots for his own gain. But whom would the Spirit of the Pities substitute for him? The answer comes in a chorus of the Pities, with aerial music:

> We would establish those of kindlier build,
>   In fair Compassions skilled,
> Men of deep art in life-development;
> Watchers and warders of thy varied lands,
> Men surfeited of laying heavy hands
>   Upon the innocent,
> The mild, the fragile, the obscure content
> Among the myriads of the family.
> Those, too, who love the true, the excellent,
> And make their daily moves a melody.[10]

The Shade of the Earth says, 'They may come, will they. I am not averse,' and the Spirit of the Years promptly asks, for the sake of the drama which is to follow, 'Shall such be mooted now?' After all, 'old Laws operate yet; and phase and phase/Of men's dynastic and imperial moils/Shape on accustomed lines.' The scene will soon change to Milan Cathedral where Napoleon is about to assume the Iron Crown of Lombardy with the rites of Christianity, 'that local cult', as the Spirit of the Years calls it. To which the Spirit of the Pities rejoins,

> I did not recognise it here, forsooth;
> Though in its early, lovingkindly days
> Of gracious purpose it was much to me.[11]

Napoleon's self-coronation, 'That vulgar stroke of vauntery', will let confusion loose on Europe's peace for many an undawned year, as the Spirit of the Pities prophesies, though for one moment he thinks to check the vaunting one with a whisper of warning in his ear:

> Lieutenant Bonaparte,
> Would it not seemlier be to shut thy heart
> To these unhealthy splendours? — helmet thee
> For her thou swar'st-to first, fair Liberty?

But to no avail. The aged Spirit of the Years rebukes him:

>   Officious sprite,
> Thou art young, and dost not heed the Cause of things . . .
> Else wouldst thou not have hailed the Emperor,
> Whose acts do but outshape Its governing.[12]

After all, as the aged Spirit of the Years caustically observes, the Spirit of the Pities is 'a mere juvenile — who only came into being in what the earthlings call their Tertiary Age!' So Europe is swept at once with well-based alarms, and especially England, where voices are raised:

> 'Where, where is Nelson?' questions every tongue; —
> 'How views he so unparalleled a scheme?'[13]

The action then switches to the British Fleet at Gibraltar, sweeping into the campaign of Trafalgar.

It has frequently been pointed out how well adapted the character of Napoleon and the Napoleonic Wars were to Hardy's poetic genius, providing as they do (and as Tolstoy also perceived) perhaps the best of all historical 'models' for a deterministic philosophy. Much is made of Napoleon's own consciousness of himself as a 'fated' figure —

> Some force within me, baffling mine intent,
> Harries me onward, whether I will or no.
> My star, my star is what's to blame — not I.
> It is unswervable![14]

and of his wars as a gigantic puppet-show with nations and armies appearing like huge machines or caterpillars in a flux of somnambulistic activity. This is all true enough so long as it is not imagined that Hardy chose his theme out of regard for its philosophic possibilities. Quite apart from the fact that his theme rather chose him than he it, and that he never tired of insisting that any doctrines put forward by his Spirit Intelligences were 'but tentative, and are advanced with little eye to a clear metaphysic, or systemized philosophy', to advance any such notion would be to succumb to the 'intellectual fallacy'. The so-called philosophy is nothing more than a technical device for telling effectively the kind of story that the poet wants to tell for reasons of personal temperament and experience. As always with the poet, the artistic form preceded and directed the metaphysic rather that *vice versa.* It might be supposed that when the metaphysic obtrudes unduly, as it frequently does in the commentary of the Spirits, there would ensue a certain failure of poetic power in favour of didacticism. Yet this rarely happens, so completely has Hardy realised his Phantom Intelligences, an achievement in keeping with his temperamental affiliations. All his life he had traffic with ghosts, as only a countryman can, and one of the most popular words in his poetry is 'phantom'. The best way of getting a melancholy satisfaction out of life, he once said, was to die before one was out of the flesh, and we read in the *Life:*

> Hence even when I enter a room to pay a simple morning call I have unconsciously the habit of regarding the scene as if I were a spectre not solid enough to influence my environment; only fit to behold and say, as another spectre said: 'Peace be unto you!'[15]

Hardy wanted not merely to see a ghost but to be one. And why not? It should not have been difficult for a man who, according to his own account, had seen souls outside bodies at a concert in Prince's Hall and in the British Museum Reading Room. The Phantom Intelligences in *The Dynasts* are as lively and differentiated personages as any of the 'real' characters: amused and amusing, sardonic and sometimes schoolmasterly. They supply the light relief, along with the Wessex countryfolk. There is no need to take them at all solemnly.

> This tale of Will
> And Life's impulsion by Incognizance
> I cannot take[16]

says that Hardyesque character, the Spirit of the Pities. 'Nor can I', said Sir Max Beerbohm in an otherwise enthusiastic review.[17] The historian more often joins the Spirit Ironic when he casts the balance at the end of the drama:

> Nothing care I for these high-doctrined dreams,
> And shape the case in quite a common way,
> So I would ask, Ajaccian Bonaparte,
> Has all this been worth while?[18]

Indeed, it must seem that Hardy has departed far from the historian's course, The historian is not concerned with the Immanent Will and Its Designs, and gets on very well without them. Hence *The Dynasts* has rarely appeared in any historical bibliography of works on the Napoleonic Age. Herbert Fisher's *Napoleon* puts it at the top of a section called 'General Literature', along with Meredith, Victor Hugo and Anatole France. Schoolmasters who were preparing boys for university scholarship examinations used to include it in a list similarly headed, and many a youngster competing for an award in History used to plough his way through at least the sections on Trafalgar and Waterloo. It is very unlikely that they do so still, or that they will do so ever again. *The Dynasts* is reserved for adult minds.

Hardy, who in so many ways was ahead of his time, might almost have written *The Dynasts* as a radio-drama, and it is not surprising that it has been such a success as broadcasting material. When Hardy writes of the

> Monotonic delivery of speeches, with dreamy conventional gestures, something in the manner traditionally maintained by the old Christmas mummers, the curiously hypnotising impressiveness of whose automatic style — that of persons who spoke by no will of their own — may be remembered by all who ever experienced it . . .[19]

he might, except for the part played by a gesture, be writing of a radio performance. Mumming and broadcasting: a conjunction of ancient and modern typical of Hardy.

Once more we are back on Egdon Heath where the old Christmas Mummers consisted of local hearts and heads. Upon this ancient stock he grafted the pictorial imagery

culled from books that Egdon never knew by men who knew
not Egdon. His capacity for taking and shaping from such
sources what his imaginative genius required was uncanny. It
was assisted by the imaginative gifts of the historians
themselves. Some of the finest writing in *The Dynasts,* as Dr
Clifford has shown, was fired by what he read of these
writers, although by no means all. The most striking instances
are to be found in the battle-scenes. There are half a dozen
battles, in five of which English forces had no part, where
Hardy evidently found the accounts of the historians
could afford him detail that he would be unlikely
to obtain in person: these five were all fought in Eastern
Europe or in Russia. The topography of snow-covered lands,
lands of lakes and pine-forests and extensive plains, presented
problems of description to an English poet. It is possible to
show that he made use of words and images from historians
here, as Dr Clifford has shown, but it may be seen from an
examination of the details indicated in the chart attached to
her work that it was hardly ever a matter of paraphrasing the
historical works. The closest approximation to an 'authority'
is Hardy's use of Siborne's account of the advance of Ney's
cavalry at Waterloo. The inner life and significance of this
famous passage in *The Dynasts* (Part 3, Act VII, Scene iv) is
totally absent in Siborne, while the lines abound in the
unmistakable strokes of Hardy's poetic mind. Strongly
emotional word-painters like Gleig, Hazlitt and Sloane show
through certain passages he wrote on Leipzig. There was
nothing for Hardy, however, to learn from even these writers
about men falling like grass before the scythe or the air being
full of severed limbs. As for the likening of an army's voice to
the drone of an organ with the pedal continuously pressed
down, the simile came readily to the 'churchy' Hardy of
Stinsford parish. Scythes and organs, even men frozen to
death, were familiar furnishings to a countryman.

One source, however, Hardy often uses almost word for
word: the Reports of Parliamentary Debates. There was no
'Hansard' until 1812. Before that time we are dependent
upon Cobbett's 'Parliamentary History', which was gathered
from many sources and was often defective. In addition to

this, Hardy had the annual summaries in *The Annual Register*. The inadequacy of verbatim reporting of the House of Commons cannot be said to have hampered him. Even in the days before John Wilkes succeeded in securing the relaxation of the House of Commons' ban on reporting in the case of Brass Crosby (1771), a writer of resource and imagination like Samuel Johnson could 'report' debates in the House collusively. The third Scene of Part 1 of *The Dynasts* is entitled LONDON. THE OLD HOUSE OF COMMONS, and the stage-directions give a careful and quite accurate description of the Chamber before it was rebuilt after the fire of 1834. Hardy was born too late to see the old House at St Stephen's, an overcrowded pit, or den, 80 by 40 feet in size, and only 30 feet high, lighted by oil-lamps and lined with tapestries. When he first saw London on a visit with his mother in the eighteen-forties, the gothic palace of Barry and Pugin was still incomplete and the Commons resided temporarily in the old House of Lords. He could see the old House, however, in the familiar Hickel engraving which showed the faithful Commons crouching beneath the spell of the Younger Pitt like a covey of partridges beneath the wings of a hawk. There are eight pages of debate in Act I, Scene iii of Part 1. The motion concerns the defence of the Realm, which Sheridan calls 'Mr. Pitt's new Patent Parish Pill'. Pitt, Sheridan, Windham, Whitbread, Bathurst, Fox and others speak at some length, while the Spirits supply an ironic commentary. The Spirit of the Pities groans,

> It irks me that they thus should Yea and Nay
> As though a power lay in their oraclings.

All the same it is admitted that the 'oraclings' of 'this thwart parliament . . . so insular, empiric, un-ideal . . . may figure forth . . . its legend large on History . . . ' if only because it was near the last time when 'this man Pitt' was there.

> The ritual of each party is rehearsed,
> Dislodging not one vote or prejudice;
> The ministers their ministries retain,
> And Ins as Ins, and Outs as Outs, remain.

But as a good Victorian Liberal or Radical, Hardy could not

be wholly sceptical about the value of parliamentary institutions or failing in respect for the great figures of the parliamentary tradition. Attending Palmerston's funeral in 1865 (or as he wrote to his sister, Mary; seeing Lord Palmerston 'lowered into the grave'), he remembered how he had heard him speak in the House of Commons shortly before. Palmerston had been War Secretary during the hostilities described in *The Dynasts,* and Hardy felt a personal conjunction with the actual participants in the drama on attending at the scene in the Abbey. He sent Mary a plan of the Abbey marked with a cross at the spot where he had stood to see the great man interred, between Pitt and Fox, to the Dead March in *Saul* and Beethoven's Funeral March:

> I think I was never so much impressed with a ceremony in my life before, and I wd. not have missed it for anything . . . Only fancy, Ld. P. has been connected with the govt. off and on for the last 60 years, and that he was contemporaneous with Pitt, Fox, Sheridan, Burke, etc. I mean to say his life over-lapped theirs so to speak.[20]

Thus history came alive with the death of a Dynast. He had not yet thought of *The Dynasts* in 1865. It was, as we have seen, on Waterloo Day, ten years later, that he met the veterans at Chelsea Hospital. Both the directors and the fighters of the war were physical realities to him now.

The House of Commons scenes have come in for much criticism as among the most wooden, not to say dreary, in the drama. It is perhaps in the nature of things that old Commons debates should possess a somewhat trance-like air. The issues under discussion are dead almost beyond resurrection. The debaters, with very few exceptions, are bound to couch their thoughts in clichés and well-worn formulae.

> The Bill I would have leave to introduce
> Is framed, sir, to repeal last Session's Act . . .
>
> Not one on this side but appreciates . . .
>
> The question that compels the House tonight . . .
>
> It is incumbent on me to declare . . .

> At this late hour,
> After the riddling fire the Act has drawn on't,
> My words shall hold the House the briefest while . . .

Thus, in these last lines, speaks Charles James Fox, who proceeds to fill another column and more of (for him) jog-trot, very blank verse. Many critics have declared, like Arthur McDowall, that blank verse is an alien medium to Hardy, They have asked, too, why he did not write these passages in prose. W. R. Rutland has rightly objected that they would then have ceased to give the illusion of a play, though this seems hardly to follow when one remembers the vast amount of prose in the scene-settings and directions. The really crucial point is that a good deal of Hardy's verse, especially in the parliamentary scenes, is not verse at all but spoilt prose. Being Thomas Hardy, of course, he can — and does — rise from leaden-footed verse into short, swift, never-to-be-forgotten flights of poetry. Robert Graves has told us of how he once tried to produce an edition of *David Copperfield* without the 'Little Em'ly' passages. What resulted simply was not *David Copperfield.* A certain price generally has to be paid for a work of genius. There will be passages that crawl like caterpillars. Hardy does remind us, after all, in his Apology to *Late Lyrics and Earlier,* of Coleridge's 'proof that a versification of any length neither can be nor ought to be all poetry'.

12   Hardy and Tolstoy

Anyone who writes on the Napoleonic epic brings himself into some mode of comparison with Tolstoy. *War and Peace* must stand in his path like a lion. When *The Dynasts* was published this had been true for nearly twenty years, for Hardy could have read *War and Peace* any time after 1889 when it became available in an English translation. As we have seen, his own conception had been in his mind since 1875. The notion that it was in the air of European literature and that he took it, so to say, by infection, is one of the more absurd fantasies of the literary mind. It had been with him since his childhood in the Napoleonic-haunted country-side of Wessex. It is possible, indeed it is probable, that when he read *War and Peace* in his fifties the book came to him as one more historical document of the kind that he preferred to all others, history 'as it struck a contemporary'. True, the author of *War and Peace* had not participated in the Napoleonic Wars (he was not born until 1828, sixteen years after the Moscow campaign), but, like Hardy, he had grown up among people who had; moreover, the young Tolstoy had fought in the Crimean War which was its sequel, and one of his first writings was his *Tales of Army Life*.

Hardy was twenty-five when the first part of *War and Peace* came out. He was all but thirty when it was completed.[1] By the time it came to him in English he was drawing near to the end of his career as a novelist. Although *Anna Karénina* was in his library and must have called forth the admiration and the sympathy of the author of *Tess of the d'Urbervilles,* it seems unlikely that he would have thought of its author as one of his brethren of the craft of fiction. It is a great deal more probable that he thought of 'Count Tolstoy' as the author of *War and Peace,* and of *War and Peace* 'as a source of facts that are necessary for the writing of his work'.

To him, as Dr Clifford has suggested, it is 'only one of the many works he consults to find facts to illustrate a theme that is already well formed in his mind'. He makes use of it, or of certain parts of it, very much as he makes use of other 'source materials'. He makes notes on it, marking certain passages in his draft manuscript, now in the Dorchester Museum, with the abbreviations 'Tol' or 'W & P', adjoining occasionally 'Al' (Alison) or 'Thiers'. Dr Clifford has assembled these references in her excellent essay and showed how they apply to details of description, particularly in passages relevant to the Moscow campaign and the Retreat.[2] Beyond this she shows that any inquiry into the possible 'influence' of one work on the other is scarcely profitable. The differences between Tolstoy's novel and Hardy's Epic-Drama, she concludes, are so wide and deep that 'the only common ground between them would seem to be that they are concerned with the same period of History'. Similarities in their respective philosophies of mankind and the universe, she thinks, are 'minor', while she discerns that the 'essential' differences go far deeper, even though we are not told what they are. She simply tells us that both create a world at war, and that while in Tolstoy's world the people are influenced by their relationships with one another as well as by the historical events of their time, in Hardy's world,

> the identities of human beings, and the relationships between them, are integrated into, and sometimes over-whelmed by, a living whole of violence and suffering.

In other words, Tolstoy was writing a novel about human beings whose relationships come under the sway of history, whereas Hardy was writing a poetic drama about the victims of impersonal forces operating in history. In Tolstoy we are made to witness (in the words of Dole's translation) 'that strange affair' which goes on 'not by the will of men, but by the will of Him who rules men and worlds', while in Hardy we witness the operations of

> A Will that wills above the will of each,
> Yet but the will of all conjunctively;
> A fabric of excitement, web of rage,
> That permeates as one stuff the weltering whole.[3]

Hardy takes over the philosophical argument where Tolstoy leaves off, though as a matter of fact he does not argue at all but assumes the truth of his attitude and leaves the reader to subsume it from his poetry. He might be said to sum up all that Tolstoy has to say (after much didactic argument at the end of his novel) about the great-man theory of history in Napoleon's famous reflection:

> Some force within me, baffling mine intent,
> Harries me onward, whether I will or no.
> My star, my star is what's to blame — not I.
> It is unswervable![4]

That is one of the advantages of poetry as a vehicle for philosophy. It can say it all so briefly and pointedly.

Outside the world of literature there was at least one point on which the two great writers shared common ground. In 1904 Hardy wrote to *The Times* about its editorial comment on Tolstoy's 'philosophic sermon on war', and after referring to the sermon's 'extravagances of detail' went on to say,

> It may exhibit, here and there, incoherence as a moral system . . . But surely all these objectors should be hushed by his great argument, and every defect in his particular reasonings hidden by the blaze of glory that shines from his masterly general indictment of war as a modern principle, with all its senseless and illogical crimes.[5]

The Dynasts has its own blaze of glory.

The opening words of *The Dynasts,* 'What of the Immanent Will and Its designs?', state the subject of the epic-drama with all the force of Milton's opening words of *Paradise Lost:* 'Of man's first disobedience and the fruit . . . ' Thence, to the closing words of the Spirit of the Years to Napoleon in the Wood of Bossu, likening him to 'meanest insects on obscurest leaves' or 'the brazen rod that stirs the fire because it must', the poet chants his adventurous song, soaring above the Courts and battlefields of Napoleonic Europe, pursuing things unattempted yet in prose or rhyme. Tolstoy, on the other hand, sets out from Anna Pavlovna Scherer's *soirée* in St Petersburg, and conducts the members of his chosen families — the Bezukhovs, the Rostovs, the Bolkonskis, the Kuragins and the Drubetskoys — through the manifold scenes of Russia's great War of Liberation, and concludes with a couple of epilogues discussing the forces operating in history, the historian's study of human life, the problems of free will and necessity. With *The Dynasts* we are in and above an embattled world from the first word to the last. With *War and Peace* we are no less in that world, but we come out of it into Count Tolstoy's study in order to listen to a lecture on history and the historian. If it were possible to imagine ourselves ever coming out of the world of *The Dynasts,* we know that we should come out upon Egdon Heath, or stand with Gabriel Oak on Norcombe Hill to watch one's stately progress through the stars.

It is true that Hardy, like Tolstoy, creates a world at war, but Hardy's world is at once larger and smaller that Tolstoy's. It has the simultaneous largeness and smallness of a world which apprehends the macrocosm through the microcosm. The one leads into the other, as the first scene of the first act, 'A Ridge in Wessex', leads into scenes in Paris and London and Milan. All through the drama this counterpoint is maintained, swinging between the native heath and the fields of Leipzig and Salamanca, between Egdon and Austerlitz, from Petersburg and Malmaison on one hand to Durnover Green in Casterbridge on the other. They neighbour each other with remarkable ease, their juxtaposition lending width and breadth to 'the world at war'. Hardy's world-picture has its foundations in the earth of Egdon, and its roof in the superintendent presences of the Overworld. There is nothing comparable to this in the conception or the achievement of *War and Peace.* At the same time, there is nothing in *The Dynasts* to compare with the character-drawing of Nicholas and Peter Rostov, of Natasha, Prince Andrew and Pierre. It is a genuine case of comparisons being odious. Neither in intention nor in execution are these two great works within sight of each other. What Hardy and Tolstoy share are certain qualities common to greatness. We return once more to Dr Clifford's dismissive judgement when she finds the only common ground between them in their concern with the same period of history, though they share, too, their intensity of feeling for *la patrie:* Ancient Wessex and Holy Russia respectively.

The superior smallness of Hardy's world shows itself in the prominence given to the humble creatures of farm and field, forest and fen. His subject was never simply Europe, or mankind, in throes. It was all sentient life, from Emperors and Kings down to moles, coneys, hedgehogs and worms. His stage is the universe of living nature, which serves as a gigantic altar. Not 'the high altar of universal praise', in Burke's words for the State in its relations with Religion, but the sacrificial stone on which life itself is the oblation. The temple wherein these rites take place is fitfully lighted by the glint of knives or sword-blades, fitful and uncertain as the undemonstrative smile of Elizabeth-Jane at the end of *The Mayor of Casterbridge* when life has taught her that happiness is 'but the occasional episode in a general drama of pain.' 'Poor old Hardy', Sir Henry Newbolt sighed, 'he does so want both God and man to be good.' He tried for hours to find the source of the quotation, 'Nature knows no morality', only to discover that it was in *Tess* all the time. And however hard the poet tried to maintain the gloom and low temperature of the temple, cheerfulness will break in from time to time. Hardy's vital appreciation of life with all its beauty, its joy, and even its sorrow, is tremendous, and it is this, in fact, which makes his tragic sense the greater. The on-going of life would be no tragedy if life weren't so supremely worth while. Even in *The Dynasts* his basic, unliterary cheerfulness roars into fiery splendour occasionally, and the end comes with a note of hope:

> But — a stirring thrills the air
> Like to sounds of joyance there
>   That the rages
>   Of the ages
> Shall be cancelled and deliverance offered from the
>   darts that were,
> Consciousness the Will informing, till It fashion all
>   things fair!

The vastness of Hardy's 'world at war', compared with that of Tolstoy, is established by the ubiquity of his 'supernatural

spectators of the terrestrial action, the impersonated abstractions, or Intelligences, called Spirits'. Their presence alongside that of the smallest creatures of the field has no
counterpart in *War and Peace,* and this makes for something
more than a difference in scale. Not for a moment does
Hardy keep his supernatural spectators apart from small
cattle who populate 'the artless champaign of this harlequin-
ade.' Indeed, it is the Spirit of the Pities and the Spirit of the
Years who are appointed to sing of the apprehensive presence
of 'such innocent creatures' in and beneath the field of
Waterloo. Thomas Hardy was 'the man who used to notice
such things', and, among them, less innocent perhaps but no
less piteous, 'poor mankind'. Sometimes the humans, too,
seem to go on all fours, like the deserters of Sir John Moore's
army crawling out of the straw in the cellar near Astorga,
thereby arousing the sardonic comment of the Spirit Ironic,
'Quaint poesy, and real romance of war!' Hardy himself is to
be heard, as usual, in the reproach of the Spirit of the Pities:

> Mock on, Shade, if thou wilt! But others find
> Poesy ever lurk where pit-pats poor mankind![6]

There is compassion here whose sublimity is unrivalled by the
sublimest words of *War and Peace.* It is a compassion which
anticipated the wave of compassion that was to emerge in the
writing of the best poets of the coming 'Great War'. For
Hardy, as for Owen, and just as emphatically, 'the Poetry is
in the pity'; and his influence on Owen and Sassoon seems
indisputable. It was no wonder that Sassoon described Hardy
as being 'instinctively compassionate' and as 'the nearest
thing to Shakespeare I should ever go for a walk with'.[7] And
Hardy, like Shakespeare, looked before and after. He used
and shaped history.

13 The Future

Thomas Hardy was born and grew up in 'The Age of History', which is what (among other things) the nineteenth century (and especially the Victorian Age) was. That is to say he belonged to a time and place which regarded everything in its historical bearings and thought everything was to be understood in historical terms. Not only understood but explained. If one wanted to know why things were what they were, and not otherwise, one found out their history. History was not only explanation but justification.

Hardy saw that this age was coming to an end. Before he died the Age of History was over and the Existentialist Age had begun. Born and bred in the one, he was a pioneer of the other. Jean Brooks has perceptively analysed Hardy's relationship to the Existentialist vision, and she has pointed out how the latter has 'produced a kind of novel and drama anticipated in Hardy's themes'. She continues:

> The meaning of an author's work lives after him. Hardy has created, not a host of imitators and disciples, but an individual awareness of and thoughtful response to the human predicament that defines his spiritual successors. One cannot say with certainty whether Camus, that most upright and compassionate champion of human individuality against the abstractions of Absurdity, was influenced by reading Hardy. But he was born conscious of Hardy's universe . . . The end of *The Plague,* reaffirming that trust in men slighted and enduring but nobler than the unconscious cosmos which crushes them, might stand as a tribute from the younger writer to his spiritual father; one of those who, 'while unable to be saints but refusing to bow down to pestilences, strive their utmost to be healers' . . . [1]

Hardy's consciousness of the 'on-goingness' of the world and his longing for an end to the 'incessant process of time and change' made him insusceptible to the superstitions of the historian, and least of all to the superstition óf progress. As he climbs the hill at Boscastle in his old age, he sees the roadside rocks as when he had climbed them with the 'girlish form' of Emma long years before, and he knows that in all their long history they can record nothing but the passing of those twain:

> Primaeval rocks form the road's steep border,
>   And much have they faced there, first and last,
> Of the transitory in Earth's long order;
>   But what they record in colour and cast
>   Is — that we two passed.[2]

In this poem he sighs over 'Time's unflinching rigour' which has 'ruled from sight/The substance now' of the girlish form, and he wrote many poems whose burden is just that. 'During Wind and Rain' is perhaps the finest of them, with its lament,

> Ah, no; the years O!
> How the sick leaves reel down in throngs!

and

> Ah no; the years O!
> And the rotten rose is ript from the wall.[3]

These poems belong to 1914 and 1917, but Hardy's famous destruction of time in Henry Knight's nightmare confrontation of the crustacean on the Cliff without a Name in *A Pair of Blue Eyes* had been achieved more than forty years earlier. The annihilation of Time with its unflinching rigour was a preoccupation of his very long life. On the whole he had no taste for historical recurrence. 'Let Time roll backward if it will', he wrote in the last poem of *Winter Words,* his posthumous book of verse; and in the penultimate poem, 'We Are Getting to the End', he is concerned with the end of dreams or 'visioning'. Perhaps it was this which made sure that Methuen's *Anthology of Modern Verse* in 1921 should bear the dedication 'To Thomas Hardy, O.M., Greatest of the Moderns'. A dedication in those terms would serve equally

well for an anthology of modern verse today. For he was, as
one says, 'up' with his time. He was indeed ahead of it or, in
a more meaningful sense than that of the cliché as it is
generally used, he was 'avant-garde'. And like much else, it all
began with Egdon Heath.

The opening chapter of *The Return of the Native* is
devoted to a portrait of 'A Face on which Time Makes but
Little Impression', and this celebrated passage of description
is the *locus classicus* for his view of modern man and his
place in history. The heath is not merely old, it is ancient.
'There's a beauty in extreme old age', wrote W. S. Gilbert,
but only Rembrandt and Crome and Hardy have been able to
portray it. Egdon had a face in which 'beauty of the accepted
kind' was utterly wanting, appealing to

> a subtler and scarcer instinct, to a more recently learnt
> emotion, than that which responds to the sort of beauty
> called charming and fair.

The *Native* was written ten years before Hardy's diary-note,
'I feel that Nature is played out as a beauty', *à propos* of that
Bonington in the drawing-room at Max Gate, which was
painted in the style of 'a period when the mind is serene and
unawakened to the tragical mysteries of life'.[4] He expounds
this theme in the *Native* in the passage beginning with the
sorry statement that smiling champaigns of flowers and fruit,

> are permanently harmonious only with an existence of
> better reputation as to its issues than the present . . . Indeed,
> it is a question if the exclusive reign of this orthodox
> beauty is not approaching its last quarter. The new Vale of
> Tempe may be a gaunt waste in Thule: human souls may
> find themselves in closer and closer harmony with external
> things wearing a sombreness distasteful to our race when it
> was young. The time seems near, if it has not actually
> arrived, when the chastened sublimity of a moor, a sea, or
> a mountain will be all of nature that is absolutely in
> keeping with the moods of the more thinking among
> mankind.[5]

The tourist may come to prefer Iceland or the sand-dunes of
Scheveningen — or Egdon. These places, says Hardy, may

accord better with man's nature than the vineyards and the myrtle-gardens of the South of Europe. They, neither hateful nor ugly, are like man himself, slighted and enduring.

The man of the future dispensation appears upon the scene in the person of the returning native, Clym Yeobright. He is described at the beginning of the third Book:

> Physically beautiful man — the glory of the race when it was young — are almost an anachronism now . . . The truth seems to be that a long line of disillusive centuries has permanently displaced the Hellenic idea of life . . . What the Greeks only suspected we know well; what their Aeschylus imagined our nursery children feel.[6]

The children of the new dispensation appear with the ghastly offspring of Jude Fawley. The doctor tells Jude when Little Father Time, the eldest of them, has put an end to the rest,

> there are such boys springing up amongst us— boys of a sort unknown in the last generation — the outcome of new views of life . . . it is the beginning of the coming universal wish not to live.[7]

There is no doubt that *The Return of the Native* marks the point where Hardy turned irrevocably to tragedy. It was in 1879, when he was a year short of forty, that he began to feel that there had passed away 'a glory from the earth', a feeling that might have come to any poet who had just moved from Sturminster Newton to Wandsworth Common, Upper Tooting. It was a good deal more than that, however. What had come home to Hardy with inexpugnable force was the full meaning of *lacrimae rerum.* Lost love or agricultural depression never broke anyone's heart, and the *world's* heart was broken. He had long since discovered that he was 'living in a world where nothing bears out in practice what it promises incipiently'. He had discerned this several years ago, he said in a diary-note of 1882. That might have been the outcome of several happenings in his life — the passing away of youth, his marriage, the refusal of Leslie Stephen to accept *The Return of the Native* as a story for the *Cornhill.* With Hardy, however, it meant much more a deep indwelling sadness, which gave a dark shade to everything in the universe as if the eyes of his soul looked out in future through dark glasses. What made this bearable, forfending mere gloom, was its fulfilment of the intimations of early childhood. The world was, as he said in the poem he wrote on his eighty-sixth birthday, keeping faith with him, proving to be much as it had promised to be when,

> as a child I used to lie
> Upon the leaze and watch the sky . . .

This poem is called 'He Never Expected Much', and it was in the manner of a thanksgiving that he had always understood life to be just a matter of 'neutral tinted haps and such'. Having taken this wise warning from 'clouds and hills around' (unlike Wordsworth), he 'could stem such strain and ache/As each year might assign'. This early warning, or rather his attention to it, was no doubt the source of that 'inner radiance' that Florence Hardy found in him in 1918. She herself was depressed by the war, but 'T.H. is wonderful — with that inner radiance of his', she wrote to Sir Sydney Cockerell, 'a true sunshine giver'.[8] He had lived too long with *lacrimae rerum.*

Hardy disliked 'messages' or any attempt to read a didactic purpose into his works, and this is perhaps all that should be said on the subject if one is to avoid offending his shade. Man has outgrown 'God', literally outstripped him. The Victorian Age had not long passed away when he wrote the poem called 'God's Education', wherein he catechised him (he usually denied him a capital 'H' by this time) about his having stolen away his dear one's youth and beauty, not because he (God) wanted them, but in order to throw them carelessly away. 'We call that cruelty', Hardy tells him, and 'he' admits that the thought is new to him. 'Forsooth, though I men's master be,' he confesses, 'Theirs is the teaching mind!' At the end of *The Dynasts,* he (now dignified as 'the Immanent Will') has not by any means completed his education, though there is a distinct chance that he may some day when deliverance shall be 'offered from the darts that were,/Consciousness the Will informing, till It [with a capital letter now] fashion all things fair'. Hardy's 'far-off

Divine Event' towards which the whole Creation moves, is terribly far off.

He rarely indulged in contempt for his fellow-sojourners in a sorry world. A rare exception is that cheery optimist among his fellow-poets, Browning. The longer he lived, he wrote once to Edmund Gosse, the more puzzling he found Browning's literary character: '*the* literary puzzle of the 19th century. How could smug Christian optimism worthy of a dissenting grocer find a place inside a man who was so vast a seer and feeler when on neutral ground?' Browning was less than thirty years older than Hardy, and his life course among the books which undermined the religious certainty of thinking men in the reign of Queen Victoria was much the same as Hardy's 'I have been looking for God 50 years', Hardy wrote in his diary in 1890, 'and I think that if he had existed I should have discovered him', adding that by 'God' he meant 'an external personality' which was the 'only true meaning of the word'. The search had gone on for half a century, and was to go on for another thirty years. It was to dishonour the human mind and spirit to pretend discovery where it was not. How poignantly he felt the failure is everywhere evident in his prose and poetry. We find it in the earliest of his novels and in the moving lines of 'The Impercipient' in his first book of verse. It appears again repeatedly, most memorably perhaps in the last lines of 'The Oxen':

> I should go with him in the gloom,
> Hoping it might be so.

And it is there again on that day late in his life when he told a newspaper that he thought that the best hope for the future lay in a true revival of the Anglican Church. He went to church to the end of his days, loving to hear the old hymns and music. He was, as he said, always a 'churchy' man, even when he had long ceased to be a believing Christian. The Church belonged to his social mores. His earthly remains were to lie in Westminster Abbey, his heart in the Stinsford churchyard.

When Hardy said that man had outgrown God and that God's education had lagged behind that of his creatures, he was giving very un-Victorian expression to what has become a commonplace of evolutionary science. If he had left 'God' out of it, and stuck to 'Nature', his reputation in that respect would have closely resembled that of Tennyson. He once said:

> We have reached a degree of intelligence which Nature never contemplated when framing her laws, and for which she consequently has provided no adequate satisfactions ... This planet does not supply the materials for happiness to higher existences.[9]

It was a woeful fact that the human race is 'too extremely developed for its corporeal conditions'. This note was written when he was about to write *Tess*, but it belongs even more fittingly to Hardy who wrote *Jude* a year or so later, for that novel is full of 'the scorn of Nature for man's finer emotions and her lack of interest in his aspirations'. A year or two earlier Hardy had written; 'The emotions have no place in a world of defect, and it is a cruel injustice that they should have developed in it.' The fine-drawn nerves of Sue Bridehead make her the woman of the future. In poor Sue, as D. H. Lawrence said,

> The pale Galilean had a pure disciple ... in her He was fulfilled. For the senses, the body, did not exist in her; she existed as a consciousness ... She was unhappy every moment of her life, poor Sue, with the knowledge of her own non-existence within life.[10]

Lawrence seems to equate her with Gerald Crich in *Women in Love*, Gerald who dies in the ice. Such a death would have been appropriate for Sue. But the novel requires no such catastrophe. Sue is dead while still in the flesh, if ever she was alive. 'If Law itself had consciousness', Hardy said (meaning by 'Law' Nature), 'how the aspect of its creatures would terrify it, fill it with remorse!'

The character of Sue Bridehead is the furthest Hardy went towards the future along a line that begins with Clym Yeobright, 'a real perusing man' as the natives call him. Like Clym, Sue will teach, a teacher being the obvious device for the creation of an articulate character. Was Sue suggested by

Tryphena Sparks? One reason, at least, for imagining that she may have played a part in the creation of Sue is to be found in the fact that both were teachers, both had been students at a Training College. Tess, too, was a girl who had gone beyond the village school, and while Hardy refrains from making her a scholarship-winner or a college student, he is plainly thinking of 'superior' scholastic attainments. From Cytherea Graye in *Desperate Remedies,* who had been 'carefully educated', to Sue in *Jude,* Hardy's interest had tended to be in the well-educated woman, but in Sue we have the new kind of woman.

Sue knows very well what she is doing. Sometimes she gives the impression of knowing equally well what her creator was doing with her. She is the potential unbeliever, the girl who shocked Jude by dismembering her Bible, rearranging the Epistles and Gospels (making the book 'twice as interesting as before, and twice as understandable'), and rejecting the humbug that would 'attempt to plaster over with ecclesiastical abstractions such ecstatic, natural, human love as lies in that great and passionate song' — the Song of Solomon. She utters the kind of twentieth-century observations that Hardy found it so difficult to get past Emma Lavinia, the Archdeacon's niece, and she provides a stalking-horse for potting at parsons. She admits that she has

> no respect for Christminster whatever, except in a quali-
> fied degree, on its intellectual side . . . The medievalism of
> Christminster must go, be sloughed off, or Christminster
> itself will have to go . . . At present intellect in Christ-
> minster is pushing one way, and religion the other, and so
> they stand stockstill, like two rams butting each other.[11]

To some extent Hardy gets it across under cover of architecture. Visiting Salisbury, Jude proposes that they should go and sit in the cathedral, but Sue tells him that she would rather go and sit in the railway-station:

> That's the centre of the town life now. The Cathedral had
> had its day . . . The Cathedral was a very good place four
> or five centuries ago, but it is played out now.[12]

Jude did not see at that time that,

medievalism was as dead as a fern-leaf in a lump of coal; that other developments were shaping in the world around him, in which Gothic architecture and its associations had no place. The deadly animosity of contemporary logic and vision towards so much of what he held in reverence was not yet revealed to him.[13]

Jude was hurt by Sue's repudiation of so much that held his heart as an ecclesiastical mason. 'How modern you are!', he exclaims. But Sue protests that she is no more modern than she is medieval. In fact, she is more ancient. 'You ought to have learn Classic', she tells him. 'Gothic is barbarous art after all. Pugin was wrong, and Wren was right.' The Norman details of Christminster were 'the grotesque childishness of uncouth people trying to imitate the vanished Roman forms . . . ' And in reply to Jude's assertion that she is like one of the women of some grand old civilisation rather than someone living in a Christian country, she replies, much later, in words which confirm his imaginings:

> I feel that we have returned to Greek joyousness, and have blinded ourselves to sickness and sorrow, and have forgotten what twenty-five centuries have taught the race since their time . . . [14]

But, of course, it is Sue who finally loses her sense of joyousness and grotesquely returns to the joyless bed of Phillotson. Her worship of the naked Greek figures and her scorn at Christianity are finally shown to be superficial, and a puritanical sense of sin and penance overcomes her, as it did Clym. D. H. Lawrence, who shouted so many things that Hardy merely whispered, sees Sue's tragedy as

> The result of over-development of one principle of human life at the expense of the other; an over-balancing; a laying of all the stress on the Male, the Love, the Spirit, the Mind, the Consciousness; a denying, a blaspheming against the Female, the Law, the Soul, the Senses, the Feelings.[15]

Sue cracks because of this lack of balance, unlike Marty South who remains faithful to the end. Jude cracks, too, torn between the 'complete and substantial female animal' and the intellectual woman who is not true to her own feelings. In Hardy himself the struggle was ever between the intellect and the feelings.

Jude is the most rootless of Hardy's greater novels and it is Hardy's closing comment in the novels on a society which increasingly feels the 'ache of modernism'. a society in which the 'new man' and the 'new woman' search for a so-called fulfilment in a world which will for ever deny it to them, if only because they are so self-consciously looking for it. We have come a long way from Gabriel Oak to a Jude whose ending is despair. Hardy would certainly have seen an alarming tendency to over-balance in the world of the 1970s, and, looking back, he might have remembered the fear he expressed in his Apology to *Late Lyrics and Earlier* in 1922:

> Whether owing to the barbarizing of taste in the younger minds by the dark madness of the late war, the unabashed cultivation of selfishness in all classes, the plethoric growth of knowledge simultaneously with the stunting of wisdom, 'a degrading thirst after outrageous stimulation' (to quote Wordsworth again), or from any other cause, we seem threatened with a new Dark Age.

But the conclusion of the Apology is not without hope, and the depression of the closing chapters of *Jude* is not typical of Hardy. The dominating impression left with us by a reading of his work is that men are indeed nobler than the 'unconscious cosmos which crushes them', and that loving-kindness — his favourite word — will prevail. And at the same time as man is made more tragic he is made more noble by Hardy's vision of him against the backcloth of history.

Notes

1. References are to the Wessex Edition of the novels, short stories and *The Dynasts*.
2. The following abbreviations are used:
   Life Florence Emily Hardy, *The Life of Thomas Hardy* (London, 1962).
   Collected Poems Thomas Hardy, *The Collected Poems of Thomas Hardy* (London, 1930, last reprinted 1972).

Chapter 1

1. Edmund Blunden, *Thomas Hardy* (London, 1941) p. 271.
2. H. Orel (ed.), *Thomas Hardy's Personal Writings* (London, 1967) p. 181.
3. *The Mayor of Casterbridge*, p. 80.
4. Ibid., p. 82
5. *A Changed Man*, pp. 175-6.
6. Ibid., p. 178.
7. Evan Charteris, *The Life and Letters of Sir Edmund Gosse* (London, 1913) p. 201.
8. See Orel, op. cit., p. 100.

Chapter 2

1. *Life*, p. 230.
2. Ibid., p. 176.
3. Ibid., p. 220.
4. Ibid., p. 153.
5. Ibid., p. 48.
6. Ibid., p. 225.
7. Ibid., p. 52.

8. Ibid., p. 179.
9. Ibid., p. 211.
10. Ibid., p. 213.
11. Ibid., p. 155.
12. Ibid., p. 55.
13. Ibid., p. 177.
14. Ibid., p. 286.
15. Ibid., p. 217.
16. Ibid., p. 185.

Chapter 3

1. *Life*, p. 214.
2. Blunden, op. cit., pp. 69 and 78.
3. *Life*, p. 451.
4. *Collected Poems*, p. 846.
5. *Life*, p. 148.
6. Ibid., p. 172.
7. Ibid., p. 236.
8. See *Life*, p. 107: 'He has read well who has learnt that there is more to read outside books than in them.'
9. *Life*, p. 16.
10. Ibid., p. 202.
11. Ibid., p. 235.
12. *Collected Poems*, p. 846.
13. Ibid., p. 407.
14. Blunden, op. cit., p. 3.
15. *Collected Poems*, p. 408.

Chapter 4

1. D. H. Lawrence, *The Rainbow* (Penguin edition) pp. 8-9.
2. Ibid., pp. 8-9.
3. D. H. Lawrence, *Phoenix* (London, 1961) pp. 136-7.
4. Ibid., p. 818.
5. D. H. Lawrence, *Phoenix* (London, 1968) p. 552.
6. D. H. Lawrence, *Phoenix* (London, 1961) p. 7.
7. *Collected Poems*, p. 521.

8. Ibid., p. 446.
9. *Life,* p. 172.
10. D. H. Lawrence, *Phoenix* (London, 1961) p. 819.
11. *Life,* pp. 207-8.

Chapter 5

1. *Life,* p. 118.
2. Ibid., p. 116.
3. T. S. Eliot, *The Sacred Wood* (London, 1928) p. 54.
4. *Life,* p. 152.
5. *Collected Poems,* p. 154.
6. Ibid., p. 72.
7. *Life,* p. 50.
8. Ibid., p. 284.
9. Evan Charteris, op. cit., p. 502.
10. Rebecca West, *The Strange Necessity* (London, 1928) p. 249.
11. V. Meynell, *Friends of a Lifetime* (London, 1940) p. 307.
    Florence was writing to Sir Sydney Cockerell.
12. Somerset Maughan, *Cakes and Ale* (London, 1930) p. 99.
13. Margaret Newbolt (ed.), *The Life and Letters of Sir Henry Newbolt* (London, 1942) p. 240.
14. Rebecca West, op. cit., p. 251.
15. *Tess of the d'Urbervilles,* p. 134.
16. *Life,* p. 150.
17. Ibid., p. 239.
18. Ibid., p. 351.

Chapter 6

1. *The Trumpet-Major,* p. vii.
2. R. G. Cox, *Thomas Hardy: The Critical Heritage* (London, 1970) p. 71. This was an unsigned review in the *Athenaeum,* 20 November 1880.
3. *Life,* p. 127.

4. Emma Clifford, *The Review of English Studies,* n.s. VIII, 30, pp. 149-61 (May 1957).
5. Carl J. Weber, *Hardy of Wessex* (London, 1965) pp. 116 and 119-22.
6. *Collected Poems,* p. 63.
7. Carl J. Weber, op. cit., p. 118.
8. Michael Millgate, *Thomas Hardy: His Career as a Novelist,* (London, 1971) p. 155.
9. *The Dynasts,* I and II, p. xii.
10. *The Trumpet-Major,* p. 111.
11. *The Dynasts,* I and II, p. 21.
12. *Life,* p. 49.
13. *The Trumpet-Major,* pp. 108-9.
14. *The Dynasts,* III, p. 202.

Chaper 7

1. *Life,* p. 177.
2. Ibid., p. 246.
3. Ibid., pp. 104-5.
4. Ibid., p. 284.
5. Ibid., p. 285.
6. Ibid., p. 291.
7. Ibid., p. 286.
8. Ibid., p. 287.
9. Ibid., p. 106.
10. Ibid., p. 114.
11. Vere H. Collins, *Talks with Thomas Hardy at Max Gate 1920-1922* (London, 1928) p. 43.
12. *The Trumpet-Major,* p. vii-viii.
13. *Life,* p. 116.
14. Terence, *Heauton Timorumenos,* 1.25: 'I count nothing human indifferent to me.'
15. R. G. Collingwood, *The Idea of History* (London, 1946) p. 25.
16. *Life,* p. 123.
17. Ibid., p. 111.
18. Ibid., pp. 16-17.
19. Ibid., p. 19.

20. Ibid., p. 168.
21. Ibid., p. 168.
22. Ibid., p. 172.

Chapter 8

1. *Life,* p. 148.
2. Ibid., p. 152.
3. Ibid., p. 177.
4. V. Meynell, op. cit.; see the letter from Blunt to Sir Sydney Cockerell, pp. 182-4 passim.
5. *The Dynasts,* I and II, pp. 8-9.
6. Edmund Blunden, op. cit., p. 2.
7. *The Dynasts,* I and II, p. 71.
8. V. Meynell, op. cit., p. 302. Florence Hardy was writing to Sir Sydney Cockerell on 6 February 1919.
9. Blunden, op. cit., p. 3.
10. *Jude the Obscure,* p. 13.
11. *The Dynasts,* III, p. 203.
12. Ibid., p. 202.
13. *The Dynasts,* I and II, p. 258.
14. Ibid., p. 379.

Chapter 9

1. *The Dynasts,* I and II, p. 186.
2. *The Dynasts,* III, p. 249.
3. Herbert Fisher, *Napoleon* (London, 1912) p. 7.
4. *Wessex Tales,* p. 39-40.
5. *Life,* p. 128.
6. Ibid., pp. 78-9.
7. *The Dynasts,* I and II, p. 106.
8. *The Dynasts,* III, p. 250.
9. G. P. Gooch, *History and Historians of the Nineteenth Century,* pp. 258-9. Hippolyte Taine, the great French historian, delivered his attack ('Taine's Missile') on the Napoleonic myth after the death of Napoleon III.

10. Hardy's definition of the 'best tragedy' as that 'of the worthy encompassed by the inevitable' (*Life,* p. 251) is of interest here.
11. *The Dynasts,* I and II, p. 325.
12. Lord Moran, *Winston Churchill: The Struggle for Survival* (London, 1966) p. 482.

Chapter 10

1. Virginia Woolf, *A Writer's Diary* (London, 1954) p. 91. But it should be noted that *The Dynasts* was published as Volume 2 of Hardy's Poetical Works.
2. E. M. Forster, *Aspects of the Novel* (Pocket Edition, London, 1949) p. 90.
3. *The Dynasts,* I and II, p. 127.
4. Ibid., p. 172.
5. Ibid., p. 384.
6. Ibid., pp. 122-3
7. Ibid., p. 125.
8. W. R. Rutland, *Thomas Hardy, a Study of His Writings and Their Background* (London, 1938) pp. 291-317 passim.
9. *The Dynasts,* I and II, p. 106.
10. Thiers, op. cit., vol. 6.
11. Alison, op. cit., vol. 9.
12. Lanfrey, op. cit., vol. 3.
13. Jack Simmons, *Southey* (London, 1945) p. 142.
14. *The Dynasts,* I and II, p. 133.
15. Ibid., p. 86.
16. Ibid., p. 87.
17. Ibid., p. 169.
18. Ibid., p. 88.
19. Ibid., pp. 381 and 386.
20. *The Dynasts,* III, p. 22.
21. Ibid., p. 62.
22. Ibid., p. 63.
23. *Collected Poems,* p. 82.
24. *The Dynasts,* p. 57.

Chapter 11

1. *Life,* p. 177.
2. *The Dynasts,* III, p. 39.
3. Emma Clifford, 'Thomas Hardy and the Historians' in *Studies in Philology,* no. 56 (1959).
4. *Life,* p. 137.
5. Ibid., p. 207.
6. Ibid., p. 171.
7. Ibid., p. 131.
8. *The Dynasts,* III, p. 192.
9. *The Dynasts,* I and II, p. 9.
10. Ibid., pp. 9-10.
11. Ibid., p. 45.
12. Ibid., pp. 48-9.
13. Ibid., p. 51.
14. Ibid., p. 224.
15. *Life,* p. 210.
16. *The Dynasts,* I and II, p. 49.
17. R. G. Cox, *Thomas Hardy: The Critical Heritage,* p. 340. The review appeared in the *Saturday Review* on 30 January 1904.
18. *The Dynasts,* III, p. 248.
19. *The Dynasts,* I and II, p. xii.
20. *Life,* p. 52.

Chapter 12

1. Hardy had the four-volume edition translated by N. H. Dole and published about 1890.
2. Emma Clifford, *'War and Peace* and *The Dynasts'* in *Modern Philology,* LIV no. 1. (1956) p. 43.
3. *The Dynasts,* III, pp. 28-9.
4. *The Dynasts,* I and II, p. 224.
5. *Life,* p. 322.
6. *The Dynasts,* I and II, p. 263.
7. Siegfried Sassoon, *Siegfried's Journey* (London, 1945) p. 91.

Chapter 13

1. Jean Brooks, *Thomas Hardy: The Poetic Structure* (London, 1971) p. 317.
2. *Collected Poems,* p. 331.
3. Ibid., p. 465.
4. *Life,* p. 185.
5. *The Return of the Native,* p. 5.
6. Ibid., p. 197.
7. *Jude the Obscure,* p. 406.
8. V. Meynell, *Friends of a Lifetime,* pp. 297-8.
9. *Life,* p. 218.
10. D. H. Lawrence, *Phoenix* (London, 1961) pp. 501-2.
11. *Jude the Obscure,* pp. 180-1.
12. Ibid., p. 160.
13. Ibid., p. 99.
14. Ibid., p. 358.
15. D. H. Lawrence, *Phoenix* (London, 1961) p. 509.

Index